Leadership without Ego

Bob Davids · Brian M. Carney
Isaac Getz

Leadership without Ego

How to stop managing and start leading

palgrave
macmillan

Bob Davids
Sunny Isles Beach, FL, USA

Brian M. Carney
New Paltz, NY, USA

Isaac Getz
ESCP Europe Business School
Paris, France

ISBN 978-3-030-00322-7 ISBN 978-3-030-00323-4 (eBook)
https://doi.org/10.1007/978-3-030-00323-4

Library of Congress Control Number: 2018955461

This Palgrave Macmillan imprint is published by the registered company Springer Nature Switzerland AG
The registered company address is: Gewerbestrasse 11, 6330 Cham, Switzerland

Preface

From Ulysses to Steve Jobs, we have long cast our leaders as larger-than-life, heroic figures. But in business, this belief has begun to change, and the change is coming not from the proverbial people in the street, but from the leaders themselves.

This is a book about a transformation of the idea of leadership in the past two decades—a change of beliefs about how best to lead, along with radically different leadership practices. It has already transformed the fortunes of hundreds of businesses and the lives of tens of thousands of employees—and has a potential to totally transform the way businesses and even government are lead. It has already transformed the worst government ministry in Belgium into the best.

This change consists of nothing less than turning our common conceptions about leadership upside down. As Bob Davids, who has headed six companies in his career, puts it in this book: "If you think you are special, you are not. No one can bullshit the troops. Troops know who you are from your first words. It is best if you are one of the troops. A true leader subordinates him/herself to the staff. In war, the generals eat last." We've chosen Bob's words to illustrate this change not just because

Bob is a co-author of this book. He is a co-author because his actions and track record exemplify the best this new leadership concept.

But Bob is not some superhuman leader. Such leaders, despite occasional successes, make their organizations permanently fragile—at the mercy of their departure or death. No, his achievements came thanks to a very human leader, who refrained from acting when others might have found it irresistible. By trusting his employees to be as good as him—better than him even—and letting them act, Bob unleashed the human potential that no one else saw or suspected.

Yet such leadership does not mean doing nothing. As another, inspired by Chinese philosophy business leader puts it, "To act without acting is a *laissez-faire* that does not mean doing nothing, but means creating conditions in which things happen by themselves." How Bob Davids created conditions in which things happen by themselves—and how his lessons can be applied in other organizations in every industry, of any size, anywhere in the world—is what you will discover in this book.

This "act without acting" leadership sounds both too good to be true and like a paradox. If it were truly superior, you might suppose, it would be already adopted all over the world in companies and organizations. But it hasn't been. And the explanation lies in its paradoxical nature. There are plenty of examples of how hard-driving, domineering bosses create problems as well as the occasional success story. But the idea that effective leadership could mean getting out of the way—going fishing instead of dealing with pressing business issues—still feels paradoxical. It feels like anti-leadership, and so we ignore it as an alternative.

Bob spends a lot of time fishing—mostly during the work day. For one, he says that "fishing is a great way to get business ideas." So it's work, even strategic work, because the ideas Bob is trying to get are about a company's vision. But there are more paradoxes. When he becomes a head of a new business, Bob doesn't do much fishing.

One of Bob's turnaround stories was a Nevada Casino that—as Bob found out quickly—was also a hangout for drug dealers and other criminals. So he promptly fired all the known drug dealers and replaced them with good people. He continued replacing "bad people" one by one until he got to, by his estimate, about 70% good, at which point the remaining bad actors left on their own. Only then did Bob start to leave for some fishing—because, as he says, "when you get the culture right, when everybody communicates well, trusts each other and they own their problems . . . you should stay out of the way; you have been successful when you can sit on the sidelines and watch the team win." Or sit on the boat.

All that may sound simple, even simplistic. But it isn't. If it were simple, we'd have more leaders building outstanding cultures, unleashing employees' energies for unheard-of performance. It took Bob five years to build such a culture at his Chinese venture Radica. Yet all the time in the world is insufficient if a person is not a true leader—one who subordinates himself to his people. Bob became one. He has spent also a great deal of effort reflecting on and codifying what it takes to become such a leader.

Like letting friends who visit Sea Smoke Cellars taste his aging wine from barrels, Bob would occasionally share his leadership insights with a select few. With some friends, but also with young CEOs who travel to see him, with journalists and writers. Brian and Isaac, being the latter, loved both Bob's wine and leadership wisdom. They also realized that unlike his wine—which can be ordered in all U.S. three star Michelin restaurants—Bob's wisdom has never been bottled. Hence this book.

Bob's Sea Smoke wine is radical. It is produced from the Northernmost Burgundy Pinot Noir grape growing in the Central Californian heat. It required a great deal of thinking and crafting to find a successful formula for presenting the product to the world market. The same is true of this book. Like a great wine telling intense stories about its origin and making, Bob's leadership wisdom is extremely witty, poignant, and narrative. It pours out naturally in Bob's conversation and calls for a form different from traditional argumentative books on leadership.

Hence the first ingredient of this book's formula—carefully selected and edited excerpts from more than one hundred hours of our recorded interviews with Bob. Yet the formula is incomplete if the resulting book is not a captivating learning adventure for a reader on a quest for becoming a true leader. Thus, the second ingredient: an A-to-Z book form, which we borrowed from *Up the Organization,* by Bob's friend and great leadership thinker, Robert Townsend. It carries the reader from the more basic and accessible thoughts up front steadily toward what a wine taster might call the complex finish. But the A-to-Z book has also an advantage no bottle has. Like Heraclitus' proverbial river that can't be stepped in twice, a bottle, once finished, can't be sipped again. But this A-to-Z book, thanks to its built-in alphabetical index, can be instantly accessed and re-enjoyed, or dipped into as a reference. Then, as Buddha, Heraclitus's contemporary, said, "it's neither the same water nor the same bather": Every time the reader will dip again into some part of the book, she will do it as a changed person.

Sunny Isles Beach, USA — Bob Davids
New Paltz, USA — Brian M. Carney
Paris, France — Isaac Getz
May, 2018

Contents

List of Figures

Leadership without Ego

Forewords

A Chain: I would ask young leaders in my companies a version of one of General Eisenhower's sayings: "If I stack a chain on the table and then push it, what direction will it go?" You will get several answers, but the correct answer is: "I do not know." I would then ask, "If I pull the end of the chain which way will it go?" They all would answer, "It will follow you." Eisenhower used this example to show the concept of leadership to his commanders.

A Scarce Resource: The biggest shortage in the world is not oil or food—it's leadership. Why is it such a scarce resource? Because egos get involved. Most people in top positions think that they are better than somebody else, think that they need something better than somebody else. It's economic assets, it's status, it's all those other things that prevent the people at the top from subordinating themselves totally to the people they lead. It is not socialism. Leaders get paid a lot more than those they lead, they get paid for their knowledge and skill but they are no better as a person.

B. Davids et al., *Leadership without Ego*,
https://doi.org/10.1007/978-3-030-00323-4_1

Arrows

How can you identify a pioneer? He's the one with the arrows in his ass (see Risk). The first business into a market *can* become the biggest and strongest, but being the first always comes at a cost. I pay more money to people who argue with me. If you can stand up and argue with me, I pay you more because you may be right. Bonuses go to those who *are* right. A leader who keeps his ego in check can create an environment in which people know they can speak out—and be rewarded.

Round-Table

Robert Townsend[1]: In "Reinventing Leadership" with Warren Bennis, Robert Townsend discusses the importance of what they call "reflective backtalk":

> I got wonderful reflective backtalk from my people; I remember one guy in particular who, when he absolutely disagreed with something I wanted, always started by writing, "Dear Jefe de Oro," which is what he called me. Translated it means "Chief of Gold," a sort of Inca-like form of address. "Dear Jefe de Oro: If you say so, it will be my hourly concern to make it so. But before I sally forth in service of this, your latest cause, I must tell you with deep affection and respect that you're full of it again…" And then he'd tell me why I was wrong. His batting average was about .900 on those memos. And thank goodness for those memos, because he snatched me back from disaster several times.

Isaac: The key words for me in Townsend's quote are the first: "to create a climate." This is a book on leadership and creating a climate, an organizational environment of a certain kind is the primary leader's responsibility (more on this later).
Brian: "Jefe de Oro" is a single phrase that speaks volumes about the larger environment in which these memos were written. Their author

[1]*Reinventing Leadership*, with Warren Bennis, New York: William Morrow, 1995, p. 33.

clearly had a sense of humor. But more, it was a form of address that punctured any pretension the boss might entertain about himself. The comfort this employee felt is made evident by the overly elaborate formality of his memos, combined with the combination of snark and deference contained in that form of address.

Beach vs. Seminars

When staff would seek approval to attend a seminar I would ask: "Are you going there to teach or to learn?" They would be puzzled, but I was serious. Seldom do they come back with a "takeaway" (something useful). I always would ask upon their return: "How was the seminar?" I always got "great," but never a good takeaway. I would then say that if they were going to the seminar to get away from their desk, they should go to the beach instead and spare the company the seminar fee.

Better

A superior skill-set makes you better in that discipline. It doesn't make you any better as a human being, superior to others. The more unique your skill set is, the *more* subordinate you must become. Don't let your ego grow on account of your superior skills.

Bosses vs. Leaders

Leadership is not authority. You can be the owner, chairman, or even CEO and not be a leader. Conversely, a supervisor or foreman can be a leader. It's not authority that makes a leader, it's whether people *want to follow.*

If people do not respect and want to follow the person they report to, this person becomes their 'boss'—bad word—and they become managed. Every time someone called me boss, I told them I was not a boss. Bosses tell, leaders ask.

Bullshit

General Cal Waller once told me: "No one can bullshit the troops. Troops know who you are from your first words." It is best if you are one of the troops. A true leader subordinates him/herself to the staff.

As I gained more experience and studied Gandhi, I evolved my words: "Subordinate yourself below the lowest paid employee." This will eliminate dual standards in the organization. We are *all* equal as people. We just have different tasks to perform. This is the toughest subject for most of the CEOs I talk with. They cannot take this step because of their ego; they think they got the top position because they are above everyone in the company. If you are truly special, you will use that talent to guide the team and take focus away from yourself.

Special actions to avoid: flying first class, driving a fancy company car, having a plush office… Study Gandhi. In war, the generals eat last. Lose the ego.

Caltech Tools

At Caltech, they gave me an example of how leaders supply three things for people to do their jobs. A leader needs to supply all three: (1) The right *tools* for the job; (2) An umbrella; and (3) Encouragement. That is, if you have someone digging a ditch, make sure that they have a sharp shovel. Hold an umbrella over their head to protect them. Provide all the necessary information to enable them to do their job, keep outside pressures off them while they work, and let them know they are doing a good job—give them encouragement. This works for any job. The leader's power should be used to make sure that everyone has the tools to do their job. The umbrella to keep them from distraction may be the most important.

Cars, *etc.*

I didn't have an office. If I had a separate office, everyone had to have one. I didn't have a company car either because if I did I had to give the cars to them too. No dual standards (see also Dual Standards, or No One Is Special). If your organization has dual standards, there is an ego in control.

Round-Table

Liisa Joronen[2] founder and president of SOL, Finland: If we, the managers, would have spent a lot on flights, good hotels, cars, the employees would follow our example… If I had a big office here, everyone would want to have one.

Brian and Isaac[3]: Adding perks is a business decision. They are powerful retention tools, and reducing turnover by several percent saves a lot of money. But scrapping perks is also a business decision. At some point, some executive will demonstrate that a given perk's cost exceeds its benefits. Because paradoxically, as soon as a perk becomes established, it loses its motivating power and becomes a potential liability.

Bob: A study measured the effect a pay raise has on employees. The answer: until the next pay period.

---

[2]In B. Carney and I. Getz, *Freedom, Inc.*, Crown Business, 2009 (revised edition, 2016), p. 236.

[3]B. Carney and I. Getz, "Google's 20% Mistake," *Wall Street Journal*, August 27, 2013.

Coffee

I used to worry all the time when people would come to me and say, "We need to have free coffee in the office in the morning," or some similar thing. And I'd say, "Well, what do we do with the office in England because they don't drink coffee. Now, what do I do with the office in Macau? Because if we set a policy for coffee, I've got to deal with it in Texas, and Reno, and San Rafael too. Wow, this simple little thing with coffee is going to ripple across six countries and 8000 people. So, right now we're going to do nothing but sit down with the presidents of each of those companies and have the discussion." Because even a simple thing like coffee, if you do that incorrectly, you can't believe the damage that you could do. You set dual standards and it just goes on and on and on. So, a lot of times you leave that out. I would walk in and I would say, "I'm not installing special coffee pots, because of what it does to the people in Cambridge." And at first, they would look at me and think that I'm unfair. As leader, you do not want to be *loved* or *liked*, but if you cannot earn *respect*, you should leave. I had *respect*, so now I have to go to the level of what creates *fairness*, to take the *time* to share the *information*. And if you do that properly and they understand why you did it, once they establish that it was fair, then, they put it to rest.

CEOs should expend effort to avoid setting bad precedent; this eventually was my biggest focus. I would not make tough decisions until I had to. I took the time to evaluate precedent decisions as long as I could (I felt this was one of my weaknesses, but I feared bad decisions). I was told that it takes nine good engineers to clean up after one bad engineer. Best not to let bad things start because it takes too long to clean them up.

Round-Table

IBM (in a *WSJ* headline, May 2017): IBM is giving thousands of its remote workers in the U.S. a choice this week: "Abandon your home workspaces and relocate to a regional office—or leave the company."
Isaac: When caring for employees is done merely to improve financial results, the caring stops when the results fall short.
Bob: You can never take anything away. Decisions that set precedent are the toughest. Be careful what you give because you can't take it back.

Common Sense

Common sense isn't common (see also Risk).

Round-Table

Jan Wallander, former CEO of Sweden's Handelsbanken, transformed its organization and culture. In "Decentralization – Why and How to Make It Work,"[4] Wallander cites as an example the 1st Duke Wellington, who vanquished Napoleon at Waterloo. Wellington, Wallander says, was unusually considerate toward his troops. He tells a story that shows Wellington's desire to understand the conditions in which those troops had to work and fight: "When the Duke was a young subaltern be surprised his fellow officers by weighing his men with and without their equipment—overcoat, ammunition, kit and weapons. Wellington wanted to understand his profession and had realised that if one required men to march fast and far and cursed them for being tired, it was wise to know what burden they had to carry. Common sense was a quality that Wellington possessed in full. Common sense is, in fact, not very common but something a good leader should have."

Isaac: Beginning 1970, Wallander transformed his bank from a big, slow company in trouble in perhaps the best bank in Europe. In its country of origin, Sweden, Handelsbanken is the most profitable bank for 47 years in a row and counting.

Brian: "Common sense" can have a double meaning in the context of leadership: Think of it also as a sense for the "common," for what a front-line employee has to do, and the conditions in which they do it. Sometimes this is referred to as the "common touch" in politics. It will help your "common sense" to have a genuine feel for how the rank and file have to work and live. Robert Townsend made executives at Avis spend time working at a rental counter, so they'd understand what their front-line employees had to deal with every day.

---

[4] *Decentralisation—Why and How to Make It Work*, Stockholm: SNS Förlag, 2003, pp. 22–23.

Communication

One secret to success is the information flow among the employees so that your team beats the competitor's team. The other team will defeat itself.

When I was in a General Motors Institute communication class, I stood there thinking, "Why in the world am I doing this? I should be designing cars." And I was scoffing and laughing at the class. But seven or eight years later while an executive at IGT,[5] it started to make sense that communication is our biggest problem. When I saw things fail, I'd say to myself: "Wait a minute. I've seen that before. I saw it in that GM class." And suddenly I started to appreciate the class. Another ten years go by, and I said: "Not only was the class right. It was dead right." So then, in Radica,[6] I started to focus on our foundation (see next entry), started to allocate more and more time to teaching communication. For 30 minutes at the end of every staff meeting, I'd talk about the importance of communication, I would pick out any frustration I had observed in the meeting and dissect every detail so that the managers could understand how/where communication was broken so we could not repeat that error. The error would either be that someone did not identify "the need to know" or they did not "close the communication loop" (see next entry).

I would tell people in Radica: "The other companies are arguing like we are. They are no better, they are no worse on product. But we're a better team because we communicate. Therefore, their communication inefficiencies will beat them. But once we start fighting (frustration due to miscommunication), then they win."

Imagine you want to build a skyscraper. The deeper you build the foundation, the taller you can build the skyscraper. The foundation in business is communication within the culture. Never underestimate the importance of good communication. It may be the most important thing a CEO does.

Now, 40 years later, I'm sitting here saying that all my success in business is based on that GM class (see Stifling GM).

---

[5]International Game Technology is a mutinational company that produces slot machines and other game technology.

[6]Radica Games is a mutinational company that produces electronic games.

Round-Table

Isaac: ESPN named John Wooden the greatest college basketball coach of the twentieth century for the outstanding records of the teams he coached at UCLA. Yet, Wooden would explain these results as a consequence—not a goal—of the leadership style he exercised.[7] "Recorded history," Wooden writes, "shows us that the underlying reason for the failure of every civilization or cause has been a breakdown from within, and I deeply believe that most potentially great teams that did not measure up to what seemed possible and logical failed to do so because of friction in one way or another from within. Let us not be victimized in such a manner."

[7]John Wooden and Steve Jamison, *The Essential Wooden*, New York: McGraw-Hill, 2007, p. 81 (from preseason letter to the team 1969).

Communication, as Glue

The glue that keeps the culture together is communication. So, the most critical thing you can do to build the company is to build the communication system. It comes down to two issues: (1) Identifying the "need to know"; and (2) closing the loop. If either one of these fails, the result is miscommunication, which leads to frustration. Frustration is never treatable in isolation. When you see frustration, look for the breakdown in communication. Fix the communication breakdown and the frustration goes away. If I am the one who has the information, it's my responsibility to identify who else in the company needs to know this. The person with the information has the responsibility to identify the "need to know." When identifying the "need to know," you're better off to err on too much information than on not enough information and to err on giving it to too many people than too few people. Every person in the company needs to be knowledgeable of these two principles of communication; it has to be part of the culture and takes constant work.

Once you've identified the "need to know," it's your responsibility to establish, and close, that communication loop. You have to send this information out and make sure that it's received and understood. It's the person with the information who has the responsibility, just as it's the teacher's job to teach. Because the student doesn't have an idea of what the information is—the teacher has it. So, it's the teacher's job to make sure that that student gets the information and understands the information. Getting the information to the correct people is the need to know; closing the loop is making sure that they got it. I think about it all the time and make sure that everybody is on the same wavelength.

Communication is the most important single thing a leader can do to improve their company. I'm very light-hearted about communicating. I go around and say, "Hey! What do you think about so and so?" I'm testing to see whether that information got around, whether the loop is closed. When handed a document, first, look for a date. If no date, give it back to the person who gave the document to you. Then, look for the name of the person who generated the document. If there is *no name*, give the document back. You can't close the loop if you don't know where information originated and when it was disseminated. It took a while to get this concept across, but when everyone became sensitive, the communications became great. It takes discipline, and time, but it's worth it.

Control

Management is controlling the things you can. There are only three things that you can control in business and no more than three. The first is *time*, the second is *money*, and the third is *quality*. These are the only things that a leader or manager can control. Note that there is no mention of people.

This is the triple constraint of management: If *quality* drives your project, it will take you more *time* and more *money*. If *money* controls your project, you will sacrifice *quality* and lose *time*. If *time* controls your project, it will cost you more *money* and affect *quality*. Whichever one drives, the other two suffer. That's the art of control in business. You need to know which one is driving and then manage the suffering of the others.

As for people: You can't control people. You can't control what goes on in the mind of an employee. It's impossible to *manage* people, you can only *lead* people. Every time I hear someone say "I manage eight people," I cringe (see Motivating, the Impossibility Of).

It worked for me in China too. One rainy day when we were building the new Radica factory in China, I walked by an open ditch where the sewer pipe was being laid. I could see that the pipe was being laid with no "fall" (downward slope) and that the sewage would not flow properly. I tried to explain the situation without success, so I took off my shoes and jumped into the mud. I demonstrated with a contractor's level how to slope the pipe (1/4″ per foot is the standard): I laid two sections of pipe while they were watching. I then watched them lay two sections of pipe (correctly). I led, "pulled" them (by demonstration)—not telling, "pushing" them—until they understood. Then I left. The staff was shocked that I jumped in the mud and did the dirty work. I received a lot of respect from that episode that carried over everywhere. I still use this "pulling" style in my retirement in the Bahamas: I jump into the dirty work, show them how I want it, assist them until they get the concept—at which time I disappear. Gets respect every time.

Round-Table

Isaac: This is fully consistent with the principle of *subsidiarity* which says that the larger responsibility social body's help must be minimal and last no longer than needed to enable the smaller responsibility social body to carry out the task on its own.

Also, "Showing how" isn't the same as "telling how." When a manager tells the subordinate how to do the job, she puts herself above that person. When a leader shows, she is doing the job herself, alongside the subordinate demonstrating and teaching the skill so that this subordinate can carry it on by himself. That's different.

Cream

When you find a new niche and that market is growing, you have to go in and take out the 80% of sales before the bottom feeders come in behind you, and then get out. So, go in, take the cream and then go out and find the next market.

Round-Table

Isaac: A now-famous book from 2004, *Blue Ocean Strategy*, argues for seeking uncontested market spaces, as opposed to swimming in a "red ocean," full of blood from seeking to dominate the competition.

Culture and Trust

Lack of trust is lack of culture. If the company has the right culture and personnel, you do not need rules. And if there is an employee who violates your trust, replace that employee (see also The Instant They Leave).

Culture of Responsibility

The human side is always the difficult side. So, whenever I would build a company, I always started with the culture. The culture is right when everybody communicates well and trusts each other—and they own their problems. I call problems "monkeys." When they *own* their monkeys they feed them, change their diapers and take care of them. But to get people to own their problems is very, very difficult.

In China, because of Mao Zedong, anybody—such as the intellectuals—who took any responsibility was at risk of being killed. Hence, an environment emerged in the country in which no one would take responsibility because they might die. So, starting a company in China with the goal of getting everyone to take responsibility—when they've been culturally trained not to take it—is a really tough problem.

A lot of times employees would try to get me to make their decisions, to pass me their monkey. I would shock them: "You get paid at the end of the month right?" They'd agree, wondering what this had to do with their question. I'd say, "Well, you get paid by check at the end of the month, right?" They'd agree again. So, I'd say to them, "You're asking me to take away your happiness." They wouldn't understand. I'd explain then, "Well, you know how good you feel when you open that envelope, see that check, and know you *earned* it. But if I make your decision today, when you open that envelope, I'll steal all your happiness because you will know that I did your job for you. You received your paycheck, but I stole your happiness. Now, do you really want me to take your monkey and steal your happiness?"

It took me five years to build this culture of responsibility at Radica.

Decisions, Stealing Them

Decisions need to be pushed down to lowest level possible. A poorly led company allows decisions to go *up* to the next management level. Eventually, the CEO winds up swamped and ineffective.

In China, no one wants to take responsibility (authority) because if it goes wrong, they cannot handle blame and they lose "face"; it was tough to change the culture in Radica because of the patriarchal tradition they have had for centuries. All of the decisions go *up* to the top. I would draw the pyramid to show the decision paths; then, I would ask, "Do we push the decisions up and have one brain working or should we push the decisions down and have 8,000 brains working?" Eventually, decisions were passed to everybody. Even the janitors had to plan the toilet paper supply and authorize the purchases.

"Authority comes to those who steal it" the phrase came to me while at IGT. No one would take charge when the leader was away, so I did. I became the leader and later when reflecting on how I became the leader, this phrase was born. A well-run organization prospers when decisions are passed down the lowest level possible, get *all* the brains working.

Round-Table

Isaac: The Ancient Greek cities were the first culture we know of that questioned the patriarchal tradition—that is, that every decision needs to go up for an authorization. Aristotle inspired the medieval concept of *subsidiarity* through his argument that the fundamental decision-making body is a family, then—when a family is insufficient—a village, and when a village is unable to resolve an issue—a city-state. There is an interesting debate among scholars whether Aristotle grounded subsidiarity in the Greek people's natural desire for freedom (in his book *Politics*) or in the notion of *practical reason*, and the fact that a "higher" social body could not possess the kind of knowledge necessary to respond adequately to the specific situation on the ground (in his book *Nicomachean Ethics*). Later Thomas Aquinas extended Aristotelian insight to the individual as the fundamental level of subsidiarity.

Difference

Si Redd[8] once said to me: "Do you know the difference between an order taker and a salesman? When an order taker gets his first 'no' he stops and when a salesman gets his first 'no' he starts." He added: "If you answer all the questions before they're asked, you'll have a sale."

So, instead of spending time on salesmen and all that stuff, just spend time on quality and you don't need to hire all of those people. We have never had a salesman at Sea Smoke, just an order taker who has fun every day with the customers. Good order-taking means keeping customers happy when allocating the product—not easy (see Hands, Ripping It from Yours).

Round-Table

Isaac: John Wooden, UCLA's famous and long-serving men's basketball coach, points to another way of focusing on the inside instead of the outside: "Be concentrated with *your* preparation, not theirs; your execution, not theirs; your effort and desire, not theirs. Don't worry about them. Let *them* worry about you."[9] Si Redd says that focusing on the quality of your production leads to better results than pushing inadequate products and worrying about the competitors. Wooden echoes this: Focusing on the quality of *your* preparation leads to better results than worrying about the quality of your adversary.

---

[8]Silas Redd was the founder of IGT.

[9]*The Essential Wooden*, *ibid.*, p. 70 (the emphasis is by the authors).

Discipline

Meetings get a bad rap because too many meetings are not disciplined and drag on and on. I always held meetings 30 minutes before lunch and told everyone to go to lunch on time. I only believe in meetings in which there are written "minutes" and "action items" and everyone takes notes because "verbal communications are only as good as the paper they are written on." I did not like meetings, but if disciplined, meetings play a part in good communication, which is the *critical* issue. Good communication is the blood of a company (see Communication).

Discipline is a key ingredient to keeping meetings short. Whenever I was called to a meeting I would immediately ask, "Whose meeting is it?" When someone "owned" the meeting I would then ask, "How long are we going to be here?" and, "How do we know when we are finished?" and always got a response. Everyone knew I had a thing for keeping meetings short. The tone gets infectious.

Dogs

Always be the market leader. If you're not the market leader, it's like sled dogs: If you're not the lead dog, the view is the same every day (see also Idiots, the Virtues Of).

Down, Lie

In his book, *Up the Organization*, Robert Townsend writes how people would often say to him: "Mr. Townsend, you're going away for a month, there're gonna be big decisions that'll come up, we are going to need to get ahold of you." To which he would reply: "During those times, when you feel you have to get ahold of me, when you feel it's critical to get hold of me… I want you to lie down. And when the feeling goes away, I want you to get up, solve the problem and then send me a memo [this was before email] on what the solution was." So, that's what I do. I wish I had come up with this one!

Round-Table

Harry "Larry" Quadracci, founder and former CEO of Quad Graphics: The cover story of the October 1983 issue of *Inc.* magazine carried the title "Management By Walking Away." Journalist Ellen Wojahn coined the term to characterize Harry Quadracci's philosophy of managerial freedom. She writes:

> The fact is, Quadracci often refuses to tell his employees what to do. For example, when Quad/Graphics's shipping department needed greater backhaul revenue to finance expansion of the trucking fleet, Quadracci handed each of his drivers the keys to one of the company's Peterbilts. From now on, he told them, they were owner-operators—partners in a new division called DuPlainville Transport, Inc.—and it was their duty to make the rigs profitable on return trips. When the truckers asked what they should take on the backhauls, Quadracci shrugged. 'How should I know? I don't know anything about driving an 18-wheeler,' the company president recalls telling them. 'I'm not going to find you your loads.' With that, he turned and walked away.

Dual Standards, or No One Is Special

If communication is the foundation of a culture, then dual standards are the demise of a culture. On my tombstone: "Dual standards are the cancer of an organization and culture."

We all have different responsibilities in the business and maybe different pay, but we all live by the same human standard. This is not some Marxist concept. It is respect for other human beings on your team. The pay rules are different because the job market establishes pay standards for certain duties/disciplines and performance levels. But other than the pay and responsibility standards, you must have a "single-respect" company to preserve the culture. Those leaders who set dual standards kill culture.

I am tall and do not fit in economy seats on 14-hour flights, but I traveled economy class because I knew that when the invoice for my flight hit the accounting department, it was only minutes before any indiscretions would be highlighted on the production floor to the rest of the company. I saw this at IGT, when an executive (not me) took the purchasing department's time to find him a brass bathtub for his home. This caused the purchasers to spend their time on something other than ordering parts for the production line, which caused the production line to run late on getting orders out the door. An hour later, the line workers were complaining about the "fat cat" in the office shutting down the production line because of his brass bath tub. I never wanted to see that in one of my companies. In later years, I booked economy seats and privately upgraded to Business Class with my mileage program points.

Two more examples of dual standards. I had no office at Radica. I sat in the middle of 75 Chinese workers. (It helped me to understand the complexity of the Cantonese language.) If someone had a private issue we went to one of the conference rooms. They watched me and I watched them and we all had the same quality office. Desk: I found the oldest/used desk in the company for me. When someone wanted a new fancy desk, I would offer mine to them. Everyone had a better desk than me.

Perks such as business lunches bother me. Often, the executives and salesmen manipulate their budget to have lunch paid by the company. Other departments get envious because they could not have the same privilege.

But corporate cultures are fragile and easily destroyed. When I stepped down as CEO of Radica in 2001, the board installed my successor, whom I had handpicked. The culture was killed in about six months with dual standards, fancy office, car, desk, first class flights and no walking around. If a leader wants to have special cars, planes, etc.—do it away from the business and out of sight of the company.

These types try to elevate themselves instead of subordinating themselves. You can see it when they try to elevate themselves by pushing other people down.

Eagles

If you run with eagles, you get to fly. If you run with dogs, you get fleas. That is, when you spend your time with people who can't help you grow, you start to think like or get perceived as being that kind of person or company. So, don't be associated with those people (or businesses). Be associated with those people who are good examples and can be an inspiration for growth. We're so focused on quality at Sea Smoke that we don't want to talk to people who want to visit our winery. We make exceptions for those who know wine—why talk to people who don't understand wine quality? Sounds harsh!

Round-Table

Brian and Isaac: Unlike most Californian wineries, Sea Smoke Cellars has no facility to host visitors—neither to see its spectacular Santa Rita Hills vineyard, nor to taste its great wine in the Lompoc cellar. It's paradoxical, because wine tourism is a key to Napa Valley's success up north and is generally known to bring potential clients and increase sales. But the paradox is explained if we recall that Sea Smoke Cellars' focus is not on sales but on irreproducible and outstanding quality. Such quality—as Sea Smoke has shown—leads to both great sales and profits by itself.
Bob: I ran a casino and had too much experience dealing with the public. I do not want my high-level employees taking time to teach kindergarten.

Ego, Generals' and Presidents'

Four star General Douglas MacArthur, the supreme allied commander in the Pacific during the WWII, graduated first in his class from West Point. The supreme Allied commander in Europe was Dwight David Eisenhower. He was 61st in his class at West Point twelve years later. Harry S. Truman fired MacArthur. Eisenhower went on to become President. The difference? Eisenhower had no ego, and MacArthur had the largest ego on the planet.

MacArthur had to have special cigars, special whiskey. Eisenhower said, "Don't bring me anything." When he defeated Hirohito in Tokyo in 1945, MacArthur took over the Imperial Hotel so he could look into the Emperor's headquarters across the river and dominate him, intimidate him. He couldn't get his ego out of it. He took from the people (see Ultimate Power).

So MacArthur was fired by Truman. Four years later, Eisenhower became President of the United States. All because of the difference between the two of them. Even though Eisenhower was in the middle of his class at West Point and MacArthur was one of the highest scoring leaders in the history of the school. MacArthur had the ego, Eisenhower did not. The problem is the ego.

Why are certain presidents such a disaster? Because their egos are bigger than they are. They fail because their ego is disproportionate to their skill set. The rarest commodity on the planet is "leadership without ego."

Equality

No one is special; everyone is special. You really need to understand that everybody is the same in a business culture. Everybody, as a human being, has the same value. Where people go awry is when they think that because they're more educated or more talented that they're more special. They may have better upbringing or they have assets, something that makes them slightly special. And as soon as they get that inkling that they're special, they're *not*. In order to collaborate and make decisions together as a team, we need to be on an equal footing with each other. That's the only way everyone will trust one another.

Round-Table

Victor Gallegos, Sea Smoke Cellars' general manager, on what's special about their culture: The flatness across the management and the respect everybody has for everybody else's job. Everybody knows they're equal. People aren't digging at each other and they just get the job done.

Excuses

Bill Harrah said, "There's room at the top of every market." How do we fight to get at the top of the market? Elevate the quality. I had enough resources that when employees needed something I would never second guess their decision. If I made the decision for them, I gave them the excuse to be used against me for the rest of their life that "I couldn't do it right because he did this." They now own the problem—not me—directly. The good news is there's never any compromise in quality. The bad news is: there are now no excuses. I took away their excuse by giving them all of the tools they need.

Round-Table

Isaac: John O. Whitney, Columbia Business School professor and former CEO of several companies, writes: "The leader will fail who permits the enterprise to drift into a pattern of squabbling over scarce resources rather than mobilizing energies to increase resources."[10] Is there a tension between Whitney's comment and Bob's above? Bob says that when you have enough resources, you can focus on quality improvement. But Whitney says that when you *don't* have enough resources, you should also focus on improvement. The conclusion is that spending energy on allocating resources is always self-defeating. Resources are constraints (or not, if one has a lot), but optimizing them can't constitute your company's dream.

Brian: I knew an office manager once who was brilliant at fighting for her department's share of the pie. She'd fight tooth and nail in budget battles to ensure that her department got the money she thought they needed. And she'd enlist everyone's help in her battles: When the fiscal year was drawing to a close, she'd let it be known if there was more money to be spent in a certain budget category. She knew if the department underspent, that category would get cut the next year.

---

[10] *The Trust Factor*, New York: McGraw-Hill, 1994, p. 56.

This office manager was, in a way, trying to look after "her people," but she wasn't driven by or furthering what Whitney calls the "incandescent vision" of her employer. In fact, she was undermining it by engaging in that pattern of "squabbling over scarce resources."

Evil

I see so many people who, when they were given the opportunity to receive power, they took it (see Ultimate Power). They have a secretary who gets their dry cleaning. They decide they're going to have a special office. They're going to have a special desk. They want to have a company car. That's the road to evil. When you apply a different standard to yourself from the people you're leading, then you are no longer a leader. You just gave up your chance at *respect*. You need to understand that you are no different from the people you lead. You have the same value in the organization; you just have a different assignment (see also Equality).

Round-Table

Gordon Forward, former CEO of Chaparral Steel[11]: We wanted Chaparral Steel to be egalitarian. I don't see any difference between myself and a guy on the shop floor other than what my function is. You can tell in the big companies who's trusted and who isn't: Those who are trusted get to park inside the gate and those who are not trusted have to park outside the gate. Simple stuff. We had everyone park in the one parking lot.
Bob Townsend[12]: You can tell a poorly led company when you see a reserved parking space.
Isaac: John Wooden writes[13] that "It's hard for second-class citizens to do a first-rate job—take pride in their work or the organization that treats them poorly. This is not their fault. It's your fault."

[11]Personal interview, September 25, 2007.

[12]Personal communication with Bob Davids.

[13]*The Essential Wooden*, *ibid.*, p. 82.

Wooden's remark reflects his specific concern for the players who were not in the starting five—the substitutes. He wanted to maintain their intrinsic motivation to do their best even if they played three minutes. But Wooden had also a wider perspective, as many of his players were coming from poor neighborhoods. For Wooden, every member of the team—any player and any support staff—was intrinsically equal and everyone's role was critical to team's success.

Exit to Start

The place to start your business plan is with the "exit" part of the plan (how to get out if you are successful). I always kept in mind: "The time to sell is when someone wants to buy" (see also X-it Strategy).

Fun Killers: Vice-Presidents

VPs and other senior executives can be an obstacle to a great culture. This level of management is rarely really needed (Lee Iacocca at Chrysler lowered his salary to $1/year and fired every senior VP to garner union support to turn the company around) and they think they can "manage" morale. In reality, it is the CEO who has the final decision that controls morale (see Real Job of the CEO) but the VPs can take fun from the culture when they think that they have the power of leadership but really don't.

It adds a layer of management that insulates the person who can improve morale.

Generalities

Be vigilant against generalities. If somebody says, "I'll have it done next week," ask which day in the following week. When they give you the day, ask if that will be morning or afternoon. If they say afternoon, ask what hour. Get the commitment, make them own it. And then, because people always think they are better than they are, give them more time than they ask for. You want to create success, not failure. At IGT, I would hire young engineers and give them a simple first project so they could first taste success; they would see tough jobs soon enough.

When doing a performance review for a person who reports to you, avoid generalities. The worst thing you can say is "you are a good employee" (a generality). Be specific: "Your presentation was good, especially the budget page. The breakdown and format are clear."

When they hear you say that they are a good employee, they think that you are not paying attention to them, you are not helping them grow. They know they made mistakes. You did not notice and help them correct them. So you must not be watching. Be specific! (see also Performance Reviews).

Round-Table

Brian: In command-and-control companies, this cuts the other way (see Control). If a boss says, "Get this done," an employee should demand, "By when? What day next week? When do you need it?"
Bob: Operative word is "should." If the boss is misusing his power, the employee may not ask (in an effort to bring the boss down).

Getting Out vs. Getting In

It doesn't matter how we got here. The question is how we get out of here. Take all your energy, 101% of it, to find how we get out of here. People usually point fingers: they are the good guy, it's the others who didn't do this and that. They blame. So I'd repeat Si Redd's Southern saying: "The sun don't shine on the same dog's ass every day." Even though your department is going good and you can point fingers at another department today and say that problem is over there, in engineering, that problem is going to find its way to your department soon. It's always best to eliminate the problem in another department before it eventually gets to your department.

In Radica's leadership meetings, there were 18 managers; they had cultural difficulties admitting a mistake or asking for help. Eventually, I got the culture to accept asking for help. I would explain how problems would circulate through all departments in the company (your turn is coming), and that everyone in the room is family. Colleagues are here to help you before the problem gets to them. I asked at the end of every meeting, "Raise your hand if you need help from anyone in the room." It took five years, but it was amazing how the team opened up. Every time someone would start to point a finger, I would interrupt and ask the focus to be on a solution, *not on a person.* We needed *all* of the team's energy on solutions. When they were able to separate the real-world problem from personal emotion, great things happened. Problems have no personality.

Growing, from Within

In my companies, I always want to grow from within. In Radica's design department, if you had ever worked for another company, you couldn't work there. Their culture was too alien. Thus, my job was to go out and hire recent graduates and spend a lot of my time interviewing.

But if you can't build from within, from the department, the first thing you do is you post in other departments. Now you're becoming what I call a file stuffer. You put up the announcement—this position is open; it has these requirements; all those who feel they can do the work can apply. The requirements are tough.

You might get one or two candidates who come in. Then, you have to sit down and ask, "How do you match up with this? Well, you're not exactly there, and you don't really match here." You still want to keep it happy, but they're not matching on these four places. So you ask, "Are you really sure you want to apply for this?" Then, I add, "Because I might have to post this job outside, and when people come from the outside, their credentials in these areas may be higher than yours."

Sometimes people apply with only 50% of the skill set: I can't shut them off. If they perceive that I put the lid on them—even if it's not true—then I'm perceived as a bad leader. So I have to politically set up this scenario, where I give everybody a shot even if I know they can't make it. It's a miracle surprise if someone makes it, which is what I want. So my job is always to grow from within.

Hands, Ripping It from Yours

Si Redd used to say, "If the product is right they'll rip it from your hands." So, instead of spending time saving money, we take time to spend money on all the things it takes to get the product right. When the product is right, then you can get margins well beyond the norm. I would layoff salesmen to hire designers to get the product right. You don't need the salesmen if the product is right.

Holding Back, Not To

Holding back means you have no confidence or no knowledge of where you're going. You're lacking vision. If you have the vision to go forward, then don't hold back.

I went forward a couple times in my businesses, which I questioned. The last three businesses, I had a 1000% confidence that I was going to win, and I bet the farm on every one. I didn't hold back. I believe holding back makes you weak.

Holding back is in fact planning on losing. It's like, "My good ideas aren't going to work so I'm going to have to rely on the bad ones, right? So I'll just plan on not winning and I'm going to take part of my effort and plan on losing." When I play, I play to win. Second place is the first loser. I never want to be a loser. If I can't be number one, then I'm in the wrong field. I need to find a field where I'm number one. When I started my wine business or when I did Radica, every single time, if I couldn't see a clear path—what I call "the rifle shot"—if I couldn't see in my scope where we were going, then I didn't do it. But once I see, in the scope, then I bet everything. They asked, "Aren't you afraid?" I replied, "What's the worst that could happen? I start over? I've already done that five times. Now what?"

Honesty, the First Step to Being a Leader

I recently gave a speech to a very large construction company. I had three meals with the owners and management. For two days, I thought they were a freedom-based company, and thought I could not add anything. Then, I started to see cracks. At the end, I discovered a huge flaw: The owners were not honest.

I saw occasions when they talked down to the staff, not up. But the real revelation came when I went to give my main address to the company at large. The leaders declared at the meeting that they had brought in a very expensive keynote speaker (me). In fact, compared to the market my speaking fee was low. And what's more, I had asked them to donate it to a children's cancer hospital. In private, I asked the owner if he knew my fee had been given to charity, and he told me that he wanted his employees to think that he had done something "big" for them by inviting a highly paid speaker to address them. He lied to manipulate his people.

I looked back and saw other instances where the owners had lied. These owners were for themselves, not their people. No matter how they try to convince staff that what they do is for the staff, down deep the people know they are liars.

I reversed my opinion: the company is not freedom-based. For that, you must trust your people enough to be honest with them.

Hourglass

While I was the head of engineering at IGT, its owner, Si Redd, would often press us to get our product to the market faster. "Si," I asked him once, "do you know how many grains of sand can fit through the neck of an hourglass at once?"

"One," he replied.

"Now, if you take the lid off an hourglass, put your hand in and press the sand, how many grains of sand will go through an hourglass?", I asked.

"None will," he replied, "but why are you asking, boy?"

"Because that's what you are doing to us in engineering," I told him. It took more persuasion but finally he let us do it our way (see also Nine Men and a Baby).

Idiots, Making Them

Micromanagement sends the message to the people that they are idiots. And as long as you think they are idiots, they will be idiots. In fact, you're making them idiots. The people who go out and make you money, you think they're idiots. Why do you keep them if they're idiots?

Round-Table

Brian: John Wooden says, "A group freed from fear of having to check on *everything* with their leader has an energy for action that is formidable. It gets things done."[14] It's easy for senior leadership to underestimate the cumulative weight of repeatedly being "put in your place" by those at the top, or even just in the middle. If you tell your employees that you value their initiative, but also shoot down too many of their ideas—even if, or maybe especially if you disagree with them—you'll get automatons who rarely disagree openly, but also rarely take chances. It saps not just initiative, but the desire for initiative. Convincing employees that it's ok to take risks may be one of the hardest, but also one of the most rewarding, tasks in transforming a command-and-control organization.

[14] *The Essential Wooden*, *ibid.*, p. 95 (the emphasis is by the authors).

Idiots, the Virtues Of

Every time I started a business and the people told me I was an idiot, I ended up making a lot of money. Si Redd used to say me, "Boy, you gotta be where they ain't." What that means is that you find areas of low competition because high competition means lower margins, and lower margins mean less profit. So we were always looking for places where we could be unique. If the thinking is out-of-the-box, people may not understand because they have not seen it before. Therefore you are an idiot.

When people have never seen anything like that before, they think there's no precedent and hence, there's no prospect of success. But the point is that since there's no precedent, you have the opportunity for success. There also has to be risk: "No risk, no return." That is because someone else is already doing it. The higher the risk, the higher the potential return (see Risk).

I was a design consultant selling my design time by the hour. At 20 hours/day, I ran out of inventory (time). I figured that I had to make money when I slept. That meant, build a product. I was designing great products for companies and they were making the big money from my ideas while I was selling hours. I learned risk/return ratio at Caltech; that filled in the missing piece. The companies I was designing for were taking the risk and making the money. In December 1987, I jumped on an airplane to Hong Kong to get my designs made for myself… What a risk!

Ingredients and Inventory

Number one, convince me you have a product. Second, convince me you have a customer. If you have a customer, show me how you rifle-shot that customer and don't tell me you're going to use a shot-gun (see Shotgun Innovation). I want you to tell me how your rifle will shoot that customer. Shotguns are good at scattering and bringing down small game; a well-placed rifle shot can bring down big game.

If you have those things, then I want you to tell me what the profit margins are, and then I want you to tell me if those margins are significant enough to take this risk or should you put that money in your saving account.

It takes all the ingredients to make a cake. You have to have the baking soda, the flour, the shortening, and the icing. You have to have all that stuff. And if you're missing one ingredient, you don't have a cake (or a business).

In other words, will we make enough to make this effort worth the time/money? Will it make more than Treasury Bonds? I look at my life in terms of "business cycles." If it takes 15 years to start and mature a business (a business cycle), then I may have as much as four cycles in my life. Is this "cake" (idea) worth a fourth of my business life? Time is our inventory; we must use it wisely to be profitable.

Ink, Free

You may need experts (see Outsiders) in getting name recognition for your brand. I do not believe in paying advertising money (not trackable), but I solicit "free ink" from editors of magazines in our trade. Instead of paying advertising, spend that money on improving your product and get your product into the hands of editors who have to fill media space. I made "press-kits" with photos and copy for them to use quickly. We did their job, they gave us media coverage—free.

Inspiration vs. Perspiration

That refers to creativity. In design, you're always trying to push the envelope, and to do something that's creative. There are only two forms of creativity: one is inspiration, and the other is perspiration. Inspiration is what I call the "brain fart." It is like, "Wow, what if we did it this way?" There it was. That's the idea. Boom, it just hits you. And then you test it, analyze it, and find out it's a great idea. It's inspiration.

When the inspiration doesn't occur, you're still being paid to solve the problem. So, now you're going to have to grind out the answer to go through the analytical steps. And you may go through many iterations—do what I call the additive logic and the subtractive logic—to get to a design solution that solves your client's problem (see Listening and Ideation). So, here comes the perspiration. It doesn't happen quickly. You have to grind it out over time.

The biggest flaw for a designer is to fall in love with their inspiration. They don't really run it through the business filters because there's an emotional attachment to it. It's their baby, they created it. So, it must be good. When you have inspiration, does it really pass the business test? Is it what your client needs? You have to work hard to discipline your own creativity (see also Listening and Creativity).

The Instant They Leave

I believe that people can change, so I'm trying to take time to see if they adapt to the culture that we have in our organization. If they still cannot adapt, then my question is: "Are we better off with them, or without them?" The instant that you think you are better off without an employee, that is day they leave. A swift sword cuts clean.

Round-Table

Jean-François Zobrist, former CEO of FAVI, France[15]: Those who violate culture on purpose should be fired in one hour, even for stealing a toilet paper roll.

[15]Personal interview, April 8, 2005.

Intellectualizing by Floating

When I saw staff stuck with emotional input in their problems, I offered advice: To remove emotion, intellectualize the problem. I suggested that they envision themselves floating above the room and watch themselves down there in that room, focus on their behavior. The idea is to remove themselves from the emotion and to look at facts. Use intellect (what is real), not emotion (see also Negotiating with Wings).

Job Interviews

Candidates have to have the job skills to be interviewed, but the interview is really about whether they fit our culture. Cultures are built one person at a time.

Round-Table

Tony Hsieh, the CEO of Zappos, once told us: "We expect everyone to be living [our values] and not just living them, but inspiring them in each other as well… [In fact, we pay people to leave] during the training, which is the first four weeks of anyone joining our headquarters. [It was $1,000 but] it keeps increasing: right now it's $2,000 … We don't want people to be here if just for the paycheck. We want people here who really believe in our culture and want to be a part of that… We have a new class every 3–4 weeks, each about 40 people, and about one person in a class takes it. And in my mind that's actually probably too low in numbers, so that's why we [keep raising it] … Looking at [our] history, it's more than 2–3% of people who end up not being culture fits. There's no hiring process that's perfect."[16]

[16]Personal interview, August 7, 2008.

Karma

While building a culture, when you get 65–70% of good, honest people, the bad people won't stay. They see they don't fit and they leave. If you get to 80% of the good-karma people in a culture, the remaining 20% run for the door.

I became the head of a casino once. The casino was a drug hangout, a very tough place. When I arrived, the first thing I did was immediately fire all the known drug dealers. Then I started replacing them with good people, one by one. I knew they were still some bad people but when I finally got to about 70% of good, the others left on their own.

Keeping the Culture

My job now is the keeper of the culture. That's my job. I do it by talking to everybody every day, touch everybody every day: "Hello, how are you, how's it going, what do you need?"

Round-Table

David Kelley, President and founder of IDEO, the world's most influential design company[17]: I view my job as maintaining the culture. That was the most important thing. Everything else was a distraction.
Jean-François Zobrist[18]: I would go every morning tour the shop floor and say hello to everyone, exchange a couple of words, see that they are in good mood (and offer help if they aren't). One of our unwritten rules is "always be in a good mood" and it starts with the CEO. I once tried an experiment: for two days in a row, while touring the shop floor, I wore a surly face. Amazing: on the third day, no one in the plant was smiling and everyone had a surly face.

---

[17]Personal interview, September 15, 2008.
[18]Personal interview, April 8, 2005.

Kicking a Baby Bird

Usually, I don't chat with my flight neighbors. But this time, the guy next to me started a conversation. He told me he was an executive in a financial company but that he had a dream: to build his own mergers and acquisitions business; yet, if he did, he'd be taking a big risk. He was scared.

I never start a sentence with the word "if," so I said to him, "When it's all said and done, you're afraid that if you fail you're going to come back to where you are. That's just a shame." He wrote it in his notes and left.

One month later, he quit and started his company.

He's living the dream, he's number one in his industry now. So, every year he calls me in, usually around May or June. He sends his own personal jet up to Reno and we fly to San Francisco, and go to his office there. I'm dressed casually, and he says, "Ok team, I want you to meet Bob. This is the guy that changed my life; this company wouldn't be here if it weren't for him."

He introduces me as the man who changed his life, who caused him to start this business. And I correct him, "I didn't change anything. All I did was point out to you the risk-return ratio, and how you're going to be unhappy with yourself if you don't do this. I didn't make you quit, I didn't start your company. You told them I changed your life. No, no. You changed your life. I gave you the opportunity to change your life, because I freed up your brain, but I didn't change your life. I challenged your brain and you accepted the challenge."

My role was kicking a baby bird out of the nest to watch it fly.

Kicking, in the Rear vs. in the Front

There are two kinds of people in the world: the ones you kick in the rear to get started, and the ones you kick in the front to slow down.

As the leader of a company, when I see persons who want to move forward, I have to kick them in the front to slow down. It's a lot better than kicking them in the rear to get started. So just by the nature of having to kick them in the front, I already know they have the chance to succeed. If I have to kick them in the rear, I know they have no chance.

Lateness, Chronic

It's because you always think you can do more than you can do. Personal lateness: I have come to the conclusion that showing up late is a lack of respect: it suggests that your time is more important than someone else's. These people think they are special. Remember, no one is special. Lateness is rude (see also Generalities).

Round-Table

Adam Smith[19]: [Self-love also shows itself in the] overweening conceit which the greater part of men have of their own abilities [and their] absurd presumption in their own good fortune.

[19]*An Inquiry into the Nature and Causes of the Wealth of Nations,* (Vol. 1), Edinburgh: Adam Balck, 1776/1828, p. 177.

Learning from Mistakes

My rule: "You only *catch* people when they are doing something right. When they're wrong, you *teach*". That's a learning experience because you don't learn from right, you learn from wrong. So you sit down and you ask, "What can we learn from this so that when we see it coming again, we don't do this again?" So we're going to dissect it, take it apart, look at the dynamic, and remember that dynamic. And when we see this problem coming next time, we're immunized against this problem now. We're building antibodies to this, and we're not going to get this one again. No one should ever get into trouble for a mistake! Big problems come when employees do not make decisions.

Round-Table

Gordon Forward[20]: I'll tell you how to end creativity: "If somebody makes a mistake, penalize them." You won't get any more mistakes made, and you know if you're not making mistakes you're not going anywhere.

Isaac: Coach Wooden's abiding theme is preparation, including preparation for failure. "I taught them to expect failure—the missed basket," he writes, "and to be ready to do what comes next: a tip-in, rebound, fast break… In any context, basketball or business, what happens after a missed opportunity, mistake, or failure is crucial. Perfection is impossible. Capitalizing on imperfection—mistakes—makes all the difference. Those I coached didn't need to visualize success. Success would take care of itself if they took care of everything else. This included preparing for failure… Failing to prepare for *failure* can prevent success."[21]

---

[20]Personal interview, September 25, 2007.

[21]*The Essential Wooden, ibid.*, pp. 70–71 (the emphasis is by the authors).

Preparation, for Wooden, also went beyond the play on the court. It included learning how to lace your sneakers properly—because you can get blisters if you do it wrong. "Visualizing success" can easily become daydreaming, which can actually make setbacks *harder* to take. Proper preparation includes expecting failure, coming up short, so you're ready for it when it happens.

Brian: NBA legend Michael Jordan—in a sneaker advertisement!—put it very well: "I've missed more than 9,000 shots in my career.

I've lost almost 300 games.

26 times I've been trusted to take the game winning shot, and missed.

I've failed over, and over and over again in my life.

And that is why I succeed."

Lesson, Father's

My father, when I was born, was a sharecropper. That's about the poorest of the poor jobs you can get. Then, he worked in a coal mine, and then eight years later, he became one of the largest plastering contractors in California. It was a big success story. I went to work for him one summer when I was fourteen. I was spreading plaster at age fourteen because I could reach eight feet high, and so they didn't need to put up the scaffold.

One day, we were sitting down having lunch and there was a 60-year-old man with the white plastering hat on. He had skin cancer and sunburns and he was alcoholic, and my dad said, "Do you see that man?" I nodded. He said, "That's you." I was shocked. He said, "When you're sixty, you're going to be just like him." Then he said, "I'm going to give you the secret: You *play* when you're young, and you will *pay* when you are old. That fella, he played when he was young and he's paying every day now. Or, you can go the other way. You can *pay* when you're young, and then, you will *play* when you are old. The choice is up to you. And the way you pay, is you go to school, you go to college."

Nobody in my family had ever gone to college, no one. So I'm the first one to graduate from college and then I got addicted to college—spent a total of six years in day school and nine more years in night school. Fifteen years total of college. So I paid, and I paid, and I paid.

Limits to Thinking… in Handcuffs

If you focus on what you can't do, you overlook what you can do. Rules tell you what you cannot do. Rules are handcuffs. If you have the right culture, then people are free to think. Rules limit the thinking.

Round-Table

Alexis de Tocqueville[22]: [The government] covers the surface of society with a network of small complicated rules, minute and uniform, through which the most original minds and the most energetic characters cannot penetrate, to rise above the crowd. The will of man is not shattered, but softened, bent, and guided; men are seldom forced by it to act, but they are constantly restrained from acting. Such a power does not destroy. But it prevents existence; it does not tyrannize, but it compresses, enervates, extinguishes, and stupefies a people, till each nation is reduced to nothing better than a flock of timid and industrious animals, of which the government is the shepherd.

[22]*Democracy in America*, Vol. II, Book IV, Chapter 6, p. 319 (cited in W. Röpke, *A Humane Economy*, Wilmington, DE: ISIS books, p.159).

Listening and Creativity

In companies, creativity can be facilitated by an "open" leader who structures the culture to be free enough to listen to everyone and not judge any idea. That means listen to all ideas and not be critical of it. No one knows where the next great idea will come from.

In Radica, I held two "ideation" meetings a year. I started these meetings for salesmen. At first, the salesmen think they know the market—they don't. The creative people think they know the market—they don't. The marketers think they know the market—they don't. They are statisticians. I found that if a salesman *thinks* he cannot sell a product, he can't. Salesmen always criticize the creative staff. So, to get the salesmen "on board," I created the ideation meetings to get all of the departments together in a room for the purpose of creating the next products with input from each department to make them part of the process (own the monkey). Everyone is exposed in this room when forced to *create*; the truth comes out that it is very difficult to create (especially on demand; see Tap-Dancing Whores). The details of the steps of these ideation meetings is another subject (see the next entry).

In the end, creativity is a disciplined process where all departments contribute; it takes an experienced and disciplined leader to milk out the ideas and get them to be a marketable product.

Listening and Ideation

I took my technique from thc think tank at GM. We started with *additive* logic. We would "add": write on a white board all of the concepts from attendees. *Every* idea was recorded; a visual on the board could spark an idea from another member. When *all* of the ideas were offered and fatigue sets in, I would switch to *subtractive* logic. I would ask, "Which one of these products has the customer appeal that would create the highest income in the shortest time?" We would start ranking the ideas. As we progressed, someone would offer a new idea. I would stop and say, "OK, now we are back to *additive* logic, let's add." When the new additions were added, I would go back and start over the *subtractive* process of ranking the ideas. These "additive" interruptions are both healthy and tiring. The staff caught on that this was a lot of time consuming and exhausting work. I think *fatigue* is part of the creative process. We would end up with new product lines and product extensions to existing lines. But everyone was now onboard, because they had the base line info on how difficult it is to create. Now the salesmen were on board. But the problem was not over.

The development process is time consuming and the other departments (i.e., accounting, sales, etc.) do not fully understand how much detail goes into product development. The product development people are usually the most educated department in a company and their work is the least understood. I found that the sales department understood the least about how much time/work was involved. After we prioritized the new-products list from the ideation meeting, the salesmen would keep adding, subtracting, or changing; this drives the development people crazy. The seemingly smallest proposed change usually means a "start-over" for the development team. This causes the schedule to start over, but the sales would say, "It's just a small change, why a year longer?" This led me to create a "gestation period" for product development (see Product Development Tube).

Love vs. Respect

As a CEO, you should not want to be loved or even liked, but if you can't earn the respect of every single person, you should quit. As leader, you are a failure. So how do you get respect? The answer is through *fairness*. And how do you get fairness? The answer is through the amount of time that you take to share the information to get to consensus, the time to share the information until everybody gets it. When everybody gets it, then we can all buy into it. And when we can all buy into it, we pull in the same direction. If we all get the right baseline information, then we all have an opportunity to get to the same answer. It takes time to share enough information, information that leads to a decision so that those people can think of themselves in your position and say, "Given this situation and this and this and this, I would make the decision this way; and now, that I see what position you were in, I think what you did was fair."

So, time spent sharing information is the key to getting respect and to being a great leader. Leaders screw up by not understanding respect, by refusing to sit down and take the time with the team for that. That's where they fail.

Round-Table

Brian: John Wooden says that "[p]eople don't care how much you know until they know how much you care." Caring in this case doesn't need to mean anything touchy-feely. As Bob says above, caring can mean taking the time to keep everyone informed. If you withhold information, you're sending two signals: One, I don't trust you. And two, I don't value any insight you might be able to offer if you knew what I knew. Both signal a lack of caring, and both are bound to lead people to disengage from you and from their jobs. Give people the respect of treating them the way you'd like to be treated, and they'll give it back in kind, with interest. As Wooden puts it: "Be fair, be just, and be honest, and you will be a leader who inspires loyalty and who has the trust of those under your supervision…".[23]

---

[23] *The Essential Wooden, ibid.*, pp. 38–39, 88 (the emphasis is by the authors).

Low Sights

Never set your sights too low. You may hit them.

Lunatic

The leader's rule No. 1 is "Never raise your voice" because nobody will follow a raving lunatic. When you yell at them, you show you don't respect them and you don't appreciate that they make money for you.

Where did I get the lunatic phrase? I was CEO in a Radica board meeting when a new board member raised the issue of Rule No. 1: never raising your voice (actually, I think you can raise it once, for dramatic effect only). This new member pushed me to see if I had ever "slipped." I paused a moment and, "No, I had never slipped." He said: "Come on! You mean you never slipped?" I asked Lam Siu Wing (whom I placed on the board as the Chinese culture expert) who had been with the company since the first day and told him to be perfectly honest if he had seen me raise my voice. He thought a minute and said: "No, not in 13 years, never." The new member said: "How is that possible?" I then off the cuff asked him if he would follow a "raving lunatic." The Chairman said: "Next subject."

If I heard someone in the company raising their voice, I would say, "You are speaking so loud, I cannot hear you."

Round-Table

Isaac: John Wooden writes, "If you can't control your emotions, your emotions will control you. And when emotions are running the show, you will lose."[24] So what can you do if you have already raised your voice and now regret it? John Bridges and Bryan Curtis advise[25]:

> When a gentleman has lost his temper and raised his voice to his secretary, or any other co-worker [he] can only pray that he has not made any idle threats or given any ultimatums. If he is lucky, he can get by with a simple, honest apology. ("Forgive me for yelling at you, Trudy.

[24]*The Essential Wooden, ibid.*, p. 27.

[25]*As a Gentleman Would Say: Responses to Life's Important (and Sometimes Awkward) Situations*, Nashville, TE: Thomas Nelson, 2001, p. 173.

It was entirely out of line. There was no excuse for my behavior.") If he has, however, made statements he must retract, he does so as soon as possible before they circulate around the office. He sets the record straight as clearly as possible saying, "I didn't mean what I said about your salary the other day, Gibson. I'm sorry. Please know that I value your work." If a gentleman discovers that he is given to rages or outbursts of temper, he will be well-advised to consult a physician or a counselor.

Bob: Correct! Apologize fast and furious. Like putting urine in the soup, hard to get it out; best to not let it in.

Isaac: As Bjarte Bogsnes, Chairman of the Beyond Budgeting Institute, puts it: "Leading carries responsibilities but so does following. Don't follow idiots." In traditional companies, people often "follow" because they are manipulated (1) through fear—of getting scorned publicly, not promoted, etc.—and reward; (2) through their bosses' charisma. When the results get bad—and rewards and the boss's smiles scanty—the manipulation turns into coercion.

Lying

Never create a false deadline. If you are found out, you will lose your credibility. Once you set a false deadline, they'll never trust you again. And if they don't meet the real deadline then you have a "come to Jesus talk" to learn why we missed.

It's about ownership again (who owns the problem), about honesty and about whether you're going to lead by manipulation or by giving someone else ownership of that deadline. You have to build a culture where everybody trusts everybody. But if they know that you are giving them a false deadline, then they can no longer trust you. They have to learn that everything you say is true. Because the first time they catch you in a lie it's over. You're no longer a leader.

Round-Table

Isaac: "Stretching" deadlines and targets is a common management practice. It is not leadership.

Making a Person Better

My job is to make every employee a better person. If we can't hold them in our company, we shouldn't have them. If they find a better opportunity, I'll send them the best wishes. But, I do all I can to hold them.

Round-Table

Gordon Forward[26]: One of the best pieces of advice I was ever given was: "Don't ever become indispensable because you will never be promoted." If you were the only guy that knows how to do this, you will never be promoted and you will be stuck there for life. The best way to advance in an organization is to work your way out of the job. So we told our people to develop multiple skills.

[26]Personal interview, September 25, 2007.

Marketing Your Creativity

Creativity is a subset of *talent*. I have not seen people who can create *creativity*. It is innate. That does not mean that it cannot be developed and nurtured (like giving confidence to use it); it needs *discipline*.

Also, your creativity has to be communicated: There's no value if it remains in your head. As stated earlier, communication is the foundation. *Communication* is a sub-set of *discipline* and is critical for success. Charisma is also a subset of *communication*, charisma is the ability to get people to listen to you, whether you are selling your idea or being a leader. Those people with charisma are candidates for leadership. To be a great leader, you need "all the ingredients in the cake" (see also A Scarce Resource).

As a trained Industrial Designer, I believe that to be successful, you have to have creative skills that are purely natural; I have not seen creativity taught. At Art Center College of Design, they told us that they could only shape and polish our talent, not teach it to us; in fact, they simply disciplined us. At the Art Center, I saw many people arrive with many varied skills; the people who made it through the program and became successful had creativity coupled with discipline. The size of the success was proportional to the risk they took and the luck they found. I saw many with talent fall by the wayside because they could not harness, communicate, and market their talent. Very few became leaders. They lacked charisma.

Is creativity important? Yes, it is important no matter what your discipline! Creativity is the seed of growth.

MBWA Is Better Than MBA

Bob Townsend told me it is better to have an MBWA than an MBA. "Management By Walking Around" is the great Townsend's concept of getting away from your desk and listening to as many staff as you can, the best way to touch the team. A true leader takes on the role of "daddy" (parent) for the employees. As such, he/she needs to be accessible to all. If the team is large and cannot get to the leader, then the leader needs to get to the employees and that is done by walking around. I had companies around the world so that meant flying around. I traveled around the globe each month (in perpetual jet-lag) to touch the team.

You cannot talk with all 8000 employees, but you can let them see you on a regular basis. In our China factory, I walked all 7 floors at least once a week; I would stop at different work stations to chat with people each trip. When I would see a warehouseman sleeping I would not catch him; I am sure the supervisor walking with me would have a chat with that person later to teach them. I would also attend as many events (games, dinners) as I could, just to show up and be seen. A lot of mystery goes away when everyone knows what you look like and that you care enough to walk through weekly and see that you are just another person. Of course, a leader cannot be everywhere all the time; that's why he needs to build a culture; see Real Job of the CEO.

I guess the opposite of this concept is the leader—if you can use that word in this instance—who sits in his or her office. It is much more important to be away from your desk (which means a lot of homework!).

Round-Table

Jean-François Zobrist[27]: The CEO has to be in direct contact with his people. Can you imagine the orchestra director talking to his/her

[27]Personal communication with Isaac Getz.

musicians through the vice-presidents, managers, etc.? I call them "parking lot/office" bosses. They go from their reserved parking lot to their office and then back. No one sees them.

Isaac: If you don't wear basketball sneakers on the court, how can you show your players how to lace and tie them correctly? Wooden writes that "a good coach is out on the floor with the team." And he connects it back to the workplace: "Is the same true in your job? How can you be effective if you're hidden away in your office? How do you build relationships if your team members never see you?… Leadership requires that you lace up your sneakers and get out on the floor."[28]

Brian: It's gotta be the shoes.

Isaac: Bob says that culture is needed because a leader cannot be everywhere all the time. Put differently, culture embodies a leader's presence, even when he's absent.

[28] *The Essential Wooden*, *ibid.*, p. 61.

Meetings, Knocking the Edge Off Them

You should knock the edge off the meeting before the meeting starts. In the early days at Radica (before the IPO), we had shareholder problems (surprise, surprise!). There were three of us; the other two had confided to me that they were going to engage in an all-out fight at the next board meeting and bring their attorneys. I was to chair the meeting. On my way to the meeting, I stopped at a toy store and purchased Nerf baseball bats (soft foam rubber) for everyone.

When everyone entered the room the chill of the upcoming fight filled the room. I took a chair and wedged it under the door knob, implying that no one could get out of the room. I said that today's meeting was going to be very rough, so to warm up for the fight (I went around the room handing foam baseball bats), I wanted everyone to start hitting their opponents now, and do it hard. Everyone was stunned! They saw the silliness of a fight and we went on to have a civil, productive meeting with everyone leaving friendly. Defuse the atmosphere by whatever means you can.

Mistakes

The more things you do wrong, the faster you learn. But if you refuse to acknowledge that it was wrong, you refuse to learn. Is that what you want? The key is to not make the same mistake twice (see also Learning from Mistakes).

Morale Soup

Every single thing you do is to set trust in the team. And as a CEO, that is the biggest duty you have: morale. You maintain it as long as you don't set a bad precedent. When you set a bad precedent, you almost can't clean it up. It's like one drop of urine in the soup. One drop is too much and you can't get it out. If you let it in, you have to empty the bowl, steam the bowl and start the soup over again. I struggled to make good decisions that set precedent. I learned to take all the time I could before making these important decisions. A bad precedent could be that drop.

Motivating, the Impossibility Of

One human being cannot motivate another human being; motivation comes from within; people can only motivate themselves. All the CEO can do as a leader is to create an environment whereby people motivate themselves—not only to do their job, but to have fun doing their job.

All motivation within human beings takes place inside the person. The only way that one person can influence another is negatively. So, your job as a leader is to create environments where people are allowed to positively motivate themselves.

While taking a final exam in a leadership class at Caltech focusing on Motivational Barriers, Aggressive, Assertive and Passive techniques, the instructor (I think his first name was Sam) offered a dramatic example. There were ten executives in the class. We were taking our final exam in a room over the cafeteria where aromas were wafting.

Sam walked into the room with a blanket, a vase with a flower, a book and a thermos of coffee. He moved the tables around to make a clearing of exposed flooring. He spread out his blanket, set up his vase and book, poured a cup of coffee. He then lay down on the blanket. He said, "You are all bright executives, motivate me to stand up." "I have been teaching this class 15 years and no student has been able to get me to stand up. I had been lifted, kicked, coffee poured on me, screamed at and many other techniques, but I never stood up."

Sam had us start around the room to take turns motivating him to stand up. Fortunately, I was the last to make an attempt. I quickly realized this was an exam and that he is not going to stand up: He would have to quit his job. So, he will not stand up, but he is testing us to see what we had learned in his class. Each member took their turn as he read his book and sipped coffee, the only movement he would make was to turn pages. He did not budge. I was more convinced that he would not get up.

I took the time while the others were talking to figure what lesson he wanted us to learn. It came my turn to motivate Sam. I said, "Sam, I know that you will not get up as you will lose your job. We all want to get out of here to have lunch," which smelled so good. "I know that

I will not make you stand up, I just want to get this over fast. You gave us the answer earlier in the week. I think you are testing us to see if we take away the correct concept of your class. In all of your teachings in this class you want us to know that 'one human cannot motivate another.' Nothing we do will make you stand up, but you want us never to try to motivate anyone. You said that motivation can only be from within and that as leaders we can only create an environment where people motivate themselves. Sam, if we all promise right here and now that we will never try to motivate anyone, but we will attempt to use our position to create an environment so our colleagues can motivate themselves, will that satisfy you?"

Sam got to his knees and leaned on a table. He said this was the second time that he had gotten to his knees. He did not stand up. The take-away lesson: One human cannot motivate another. Leaders can only create an environment for people to motivate themselves. From that day onward, I *never* try to motivate! But I have created several good environments.

Motivational Diapers

You have to take care of people's needs and a lot of needs aren't pleasant. It's like changing diapers on adults. What I always try to do is ascertain the level of the problem from 0 to 10 before I decide what to do. If the problem is a level 1 or 2, I know I can solve it quickly and not have to deal with motivational barriers. If the problem is a 7–10, then I have to find a lot of time to deal with a size 10 problem, because this person has a huge problem and it will take time to get the motivational barriers down to get to the heart of the problem (see also the next entry). So, as you are talking through the problem and going through the motivational barriers, after a great deal of time, you finally get down to the heart of the problem, and they're finally out and they surface, and you spend the rest of the time building that person back up before they leave. The size of the problem determines the amount of time you take, so you're allowed to get through the motivational barriers to discuss and solve the problem, get the person back up on their feet, and back into the workforce. I explained this in a leadership class at Cal Tech and the instructor asked me how it worked. I drew the following chart on the blackboard, whereupon he asked me if he could use the chart in his class—of course, yes (see Fig. 1).

While at IGT, a lady manager walked into my office sobbing with bruises on her face. I had a glass wall facing the main office so I placed her chair so she was facing me and away from view of the people outside the room. I picked up my phone and rang my secretary outside the room and asked her to hold all of my calls and appointments for the day. She said, "This must be serious." I just answered, "Yes." It took a few hours to get past all of the office stuff and she then informed me that her husband was beating her at home. After giving her confidence in her position at work and the support the company would provide, I asked her to seek outside help, maybe the authorities.

The point of the Davids curve: When you first measure the size of the problem, match the size of the problem with enough time to get

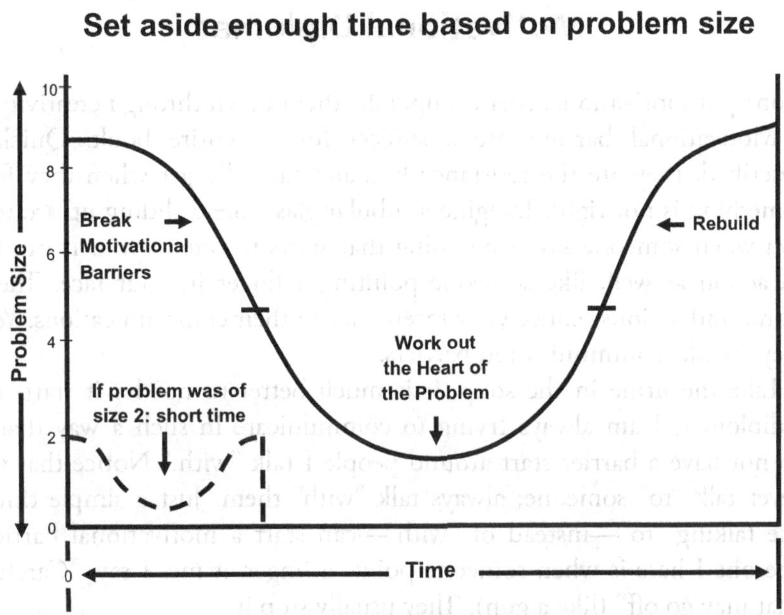

Fig. 1 The Davids curve

past the associated motivational barriers and then allow enough time to build the person back up before exiting the meeting. This woman's being battered and I'm going to spend three minutes with this woman? You can't do that. That takes the rest of the day. As a leader, you really must understand before you open the can how much time it takes to put the worms back in the can. Make enough time for the size of the problem.

Motivational Diplomat

Don't put motivational barriers up, take them down through creativity.

Motivational barriers are a subject for an entire book. Quickly described, they are the resistance humans naturally get when they feel something is not right. Imagine a tubular glass shield sliding up around you when someone says something that starts to offend you. It can be an action as well, like someone pointing a finger in your face. These words and actions reduce your receptivity to their communications. Yes, they are like communication barriers.

Like the urine in the soup, it is much better to not let it start. As a diplomat, I am always trying to communicate in such a way that I do not have a barrier start around people I talk "with." Notice that we never talk "to" someone; always talk "with" them. Just a simple thing like talking "to"—instead of "with"—can start a motivational barrier. The one I hate is when someone points a finger at me. I say, "Careful! That may go off" (like a gun). They usually stop it.

If you are always aware that you as leader are the "communicator" and you are respectful in your communication skills, you become that diplomat. You are always trying to speak with someone on equal level. This along with some charisma will greatly assist your communication skills.

If motivational barriers do go up, you have to find a way to get those barriers down so that real communication can resume. Sometimes it may take a long time to get the barriers back down (see Motivational Diapers). Get the barriers down before resuming the point you were trying to make.

I never had a plan on how to get the barriers down. Each person required a different approach. I had to talk with that person until they were comfortable. I was not an aggressor to them in any way: remember, you cannot force a barrier down. It is their motivation—only they can motivate themselves. You need to find a creative way to get trust back so that they can lower any barriers they have. I usually would shock them by going to a totally different subject that had logic that could be used in a different way that they could fit into our conversation.

If you are a diplomat, you are always keeping communications open and do not have to fix a problem.

A Natural

To succeed in life you need an area, a skill, or something that you like and you can do as a natural.

I studied trombone for twelve years including two years in college. At that time, I was taking private lessons with a great teacher. One day, another guy showed up at the lesson and he played just unbelievably. I was shocked. And my teacher said this to me: "This guy studied for just two years. You worked to reach the level you're at but he's just natural. You may want to look at something where you don't have to work so hard, where you could be a natural. But if you stay in music, you will be looking over your shoulder for the rest of your life for the young natural people coming to take your job."

Two months before this, I won the highest-level design competition on the planet. I received the highest score in 38 years of this competition and I hadn't even tried very hard. I designed and built a model car. I turned my brain off and I just did it.

So I'm sitting there thinking, "Wait a minute, two months ago I got the highest score in 38 years of competition, 11 million young men entering the competition. I won it and I didn't try." He was telling me I should do something that came naturally to me. The next day, I took my trombone, I polished it up, and I put it away. I changed from music to design. I got accepted at the Art Center College of Design. I finished: 600 people applied, 44 were accepted, 4 finished. I was number one. I could do design without thinking. In design, I have a skill where I don't have to work.

I didn't need a teacher to tell me that I was a good designer. I figured all that out by myself. The only thing he said to me that was significant was that you're going to be looking over your shoulder for the rest of your life. He didn't tell me I had talent or I didn't have talent. He just said you might want to find something where you're a natural. I had already figured that out.

Negotiating Up

In China, they can cut a penny into 1000 pieces. I was called into a meeting after our Purchasing Manager beat up a long-time supplier to get a low price. I was told this was a price just above cost; they wanted our business. I told the meeting that we would not be able to use the supplier because his price was *too low*... The room went into shock! How could a price be too low in China?—unheard of. I explained that we had to build relationships with vendors who would be with us for the long term when the product took off and volumes got high. The price they gave would bankrupt our best supplier. I suggested he raise his price to make a 9% profit so he would be around for the long term. He loved it; it shocked my staff. I then had the supplier finance the parts for six months when I could not get bank credit.

The lowest price is not always the best solution to the overall problem because in the next phase of growth that comes, you're going to triple and quadruple the volume of your products. But if your supplier is losing money now then he's going to lose three or four times that amount of money. So, he will go bankrupt and won't be there when you need him. You want a long-term relationship. You don't want a relationship where a supplier tries to buy your business and then is not there in three months when you need him. In this case, because we looked out for him at the start, he trusted us enough to bank roll the contract later, when we needed it.

Negotiating with Wings

When you're negotiating, you have to understand whether you have an emotional involvement or whether you are engaged intellectually. I see so many times, even catch myself, getting involved in a situation emotionally. When I catch myself starting to get sucked into the emotional side of a negotiation, what I do then is I reach down in my pocket and take out two white angel wings that I keep in my pocket. I put them on my back, start flapping them, and fly up about 200 meters above the room. And then at 200 meters, with my wings flapping, I look back down into the room, look at myself, and look at how I'm responding to their conversation. And at 200 feet away, it is different from being in that room. You can intellectualize the situation and escape emotion.

By using this technique, I'm intellectualizing an emotional situation: "Am I happy with what I'm doing down in that room? No, I'm not happy with my response. What are they doing?" Once I can intellectualize, then I can become a true leader.

A Negotiation Technique—Fishing vs. Working

In the late 1970s, when computers where just coming into fashion, I was contacted by a company that made electronic dispensers for alcohol, beer, and wine. Their owner, a very brilliant man, wanted to incorporate computers to keep track of all the alcohol because there had been a problem with bartenders passing free drinks to their friends and the profits from the bar just weren't there. They were trying to control theft and inventory with a computer. They wanted me to incorporate all the different kinds of electronics into one mobile electric cart that they could drive around on a golf course or at a convention.

I gave them a concept sketch of how this device would look. The sketch was nice, and they advertised in a restaurant magazine with "come and see this vehicle at the restaurant show in San Francisco." Then, this man came and told he wanted me to build this machine. I reacted, "You have the cart before the horse. You should be asking me if I can do it, because the show is in sixty days. So we have to build this whole thing, put all the electronics in, all the fiberglass work, the paint, the metalwork, welding." Though I had a prototype shop with 10 staff, everything had to be done just in sixty days. So, I gave him a price of $55,000. In the late 70s, that was a lot of money.

He went crazy and tried to negotiate a much lower price with me. I replied, "I don't even know yet exactly what I'm facing. So, even at $55,000 I think I'm under." But he kept trying to negotiate me down and in the middle of the conversation I said, "What do you think my hobby is?" He was taken aback because he wanted to be talking about the price of the cart. I said, "My hobby is fishing," and I waited, and waited, and waited. Until he asked, "Why are you asking me about your hobby?" I said, "Well, for the next sixty days, I can go out to Lake Pyramid and fish for twelve or fourteen hours a day, and I can return at the end of sixty days and have made no money. Or, I can have my crew come in here and we work the same hours, seven days a week, and we come back after sixty days and we still make no money. So, you're giving me a tough choice: should I go fishing for sixty days to be in the same situation as working day and night killing myself?" He said, "OK, I'll give you the $55,000."

A technique that I've developed my whole life is to put people slightly off guard. Creativity is an important part of finding a way to get them off of the stream that they are on. He headed in a direction, was so focused on grinding in the money and negotiating, that by asking him about the hobby, I took him totally out of his realm. And I put him off guard by virtue of illustrating to him that I could end up in the same situation. Once he saw how it affected me, he was so disrupted from his bargaining technique that he yielded. So I think it's really important to be able to get people off of their game.

Negotiation, Two Tools Of

There are only two tools in any negotiation: one is *time* and the other is *competition*. You have to be aware of having just two tools, and not to try to do anything else—just try to balance time/competition back and forth. Sometimes you can't use competition. Sometimes you can't use time. The best tool you have is usually time. Whenever somebody tries to get me to negotiate on something, and they say, "We need to have it by Friday," I say: "Oh Friday? I thought you meant three Fridays from now." Then I add, "Well, if we can do it in three Fridays, then I can make a decision for you. But if I have to do it by this Friday, then the answer would be no because that's not enough time for me." No matter what it takes, in every situation, never give up time as a tool. Sometimes you want to go faster, sometimes you want to go more slowly. The important thing is that you understand the effect of time on the outcome of the negotiation and that you control it.

Negotiation is not about price, not about all that other stuff. It's really about competition and time. But you need enough experience to understand how you can creatively use some element of the competition or some other element of time, or both if you can. But you never give up the time tool.

Time is your strongest negotiating tool. When you give that up, you are vulnerable. Sometimes you have no choice—just know that you are vulnerable and will lose the negotiation. When that happens, you just lie back and try to enjoy it.

Nine Men and a Baby

Si Redd, the owner of International Game Technology, once told me to hire many more engineers to speed up product development. He would not listen to logical reasons why his idea would only slow us down. So, in disgust, I blurted out "Si, nine men and a woman cannot make a baby in a month." He let me do it my way.

Round-Table

Fred Brooks, former IBM executive in charge of the development of IBM OS/360 operating system[29]: "Adding manpower to a late software project makes it later."

[29] *The Mythical Man-Month*, Boston: Addison-Wesley, 1975.

Number 2

As the No. 2 person in your organization, you have no chance to build the culture and lead the "fun." That is always the responsibility of the person with the final decision. You can add fun in a major/minor way which will make you friends, but the No. 1 can kill a culture and fun with a single bad policy. He who has the power of policy establishes fun. If you can, sway the leader into good policies: That is a realistic way to assist in implementing fun. But beware: A leopard rarely changes his spots.

Officer, Chief Entertainment

Sometimes I was embarrassed to be called CEO (hated being called *boss* as it implies dictatorship). When someone would call me the CEO, I would quip… "Yes, Chief Entertainment Officer," I was deflecting. But I started to realize that I really was entertaining—colleagues, customers, and government officials.

One Percent Exception, Getting Emotional

True leaders do not use emotion, except 1% of the time. My first rule is "Never raise your voice" and the 1% exception is when you need effect. If I need to shock, then, on rare occasions, I will raise my voice—and immediately back off. What I'm trying to do is to take back control of a situation that I've lost. If I've lost control, run out of tricks, and can no longer intellectualize the situation, then I will shock them, even if it includes raising my voice. But then I immediately back off and show sanity. So it's just like putting people off their game. I hate to do it, rarely do it, but if I have to raise my voice to shock, I do that. It's my last bullet.

Sometimes, instead of raising my voice, I'd throw a book on the table. Then I say, "Oh! I apologize. I hope I didn't bruise the book." And try to make some joke about it so that they see you're really not that angry. But the act takes them off their game. It takes you out of that passive demeanor that you might have been displaying, and now you're taking control back. But you need to be careful not to drive up the motivational barriers as you're doing it. Hence, if you do it, it's for effect and it's for a very short period of time immediately followed by some type of humor.

If you're a leader and the people you lead see you responding really emotionally, you stand the risk of losing them.

Open Book

I always had open-book companies: Everyone gets to look at all the budgets and financial information (except salaries). Radica was public so the info was open as well. I wanted everyone to own financial responsibility. When we would get into trouble, the staff would own that as well—which is what you want: everyone owning and contributing to a solution.

Round-Table

Isaac: We teach in the business schools that in order to make good decisions, you need to have the relevant information. But once working in many companies, most of the important information is hidden from the employees. That said, if someone asks to learn what others are paid, the question to her is: "How is it relevant to the business problem you are trying to solve?"

Overplanning

Don't have a communications "strategy" with your employees. That locks you down and closes you off. Instead of strategizing, evolve. In my communications, I would never sit down and say to myself: "I'm going to say this and I'm going to say that." Often, I had no idea what I was going to do. I would just try something. It's like evolution: If it works, then you replicate it. You try a bunch of things, you find one that works, you put it in your toolkit, and all of a sudden you start to see two or three good things that work. And if they don't work on this next person, then you have to invent a new tool and find different things until something works. Do not over-plan discussions with colleagues.

Outsiders

In small companies, you can't do everything. You might need some help with people who have expertise. But keep outsiders to a minimum.

Pay, Don't Screw It Up

The most important single aspect of leadership is probably the day-to-day compensation. The way the compensation system works is complicated. You really need to get that right. If you want to really screw everything up, screw up the compensation—it's the worst place to set a bad precedent. I think there needs to be a *merit* review and a *performance* review for the evaluation of each employee. Merit speaks to the market conditions for a skill set and performance is how well a person does in that bracket.

One key thing is regularly getting the industry's salary brackets for different jobs and making it available to the employees. Then if the job market moved up, move the relevant salaries up, independent of their performance raise. I call these "wage base adjustments" because they measure the market only, not the person. Because if we don't pay a competitive wage, our competitors will. I'm the one that offers the raises every year. I never wait for them to ask. I say, "We've got a market survey, here's what the market is, here's what the quartile is." But if the market goes down, their pay does not go down. It's just frozen.

I always pay at the 75% quartile, at the top of the third quartile of the job market but not more. You want people to strive, not just for money, but for the culture of the company. If the culture doesn't pique their interest, money won't pique it. So, the culture accounts for the last 25%. Totally transparent. Compensate your stars with bonuses (see also Performance Reviews).

Round-Table

Isaac: It's not unusual to hear that companies have to pay "top dollars for top talent."
Bob: Is that the market? If so, then yes.
Robert McDermott,[30] former CEO of USAA, told us once that USAA "helped people identify their God-given attributes [and] develop them

---

[30]Personal interview, March 6, 2006.

[and] we wound up with the most highly educated workforce in the whole financial services industry in the United States. That's why we could have 5.5% increase in headcount and increase the assets 150 times. We had productive people who were motivated and educated, given the training and technology opportunities to do better and serve others and it was their psychic income."

McDermott saw this employee-improvement as a form of the Golden Rule, while former FAVI CEO Jean-Francois Zobrist viewed it as a matter of fairness: "Real people management consists in doing what is fair ahead of any request. It's part of managing common sense and good will to anticipate the request." He added that having an MBWA was helpful in this regard: "You can't do it if you don't get away from your desk" he said.[31]

[31]"Histoire de syndicats," Chapter 29, March 2006. http://www.favi.com/download.php?-fich=management/histoire/Chap%2029.pdf, accessed Nov 10, 2010.

Paying Attention

Recognition is the cheapest and most important commodity a leader has. You have a large supply of recognition; it is what every employee seeks and it's the one that you refuse to give. Catch them and say: "You did a great job on [be specific]. Thanks!" Caution: Be specific. The worst review you can give is, "You are a good employee." That signals that you are not paying attention to that person (see Generalities).

Round-Table

Isaac: Recognition is easily misunderstood. Abraham Maslow's famous "hierarchy of needs" postulated that recognition is a universal "higher need." What people really need is consideration, proof that others care, part of what Deci and Ryan called the fundamental human need of *relatedness*. Detailed research proves it. But non-specific praise is like a bonbon: it's an extrinsic reward. Soon an employee will not focus on how to get better but how to get a bonbon. As John Wooden[32] puts it: "We all like to be given meaningful praise. But you become weaker as your need for praise becomes stronger. Therefore, it is good to remind yourself that most praise is usually uninformed." When uninformed recognition comes from above, it smacks of manipulation and can even have the reverse of the intended effect.

[32] *The Essential Wooden*, *ibid.*, p. 94.

Paying for (Self-)Improvement

I have always had an education policy (on performance and merit reviews, see the next entry and Pay, Don't Screw It Up) where the company paid for education outside work hours (i.e. night school). The employee had to get pre-approval and pay the tuition and books, keep the receipts. When they complete the course with a passing grade (all one has to do to get a passing grade is to show up) they get reimbursed. If they do not have enough interest to get the tuition, they probably won't complete anyway: they must be invested. One employee told me he could cheat the company. I asked: "How?" He said he could get reimbursed and go to another company. I replied that the company's interest was in making them a better person: "How were we cheated?" Never got a good answer to the question. I am happy to say that my companies have paid a lot and many people have degrees now (one Ph.D.).

Performance Reviews

Every review should be 50/50 (especially in this litigious environment); which means the first half itemizes specific achievements by name (show that you are watching). The second half of any review should map out a path to improve and grow. When I had an employee who did everything right and it was tough for me to find something to improve, I went to my standby: *education.* I would suggest specific courses to help them grow. We all need more education.

Personnel Chances

I have to admit that I always gave too many second chances. It was a mistake I usually made. If I did my career over again, I would make personnel decisions faster. Because one of the things that happens is when there's a bad egg in the barrel, the other people in the barrel are watching to see how long it takes the leader to clean up the barrel.

Round-Table

Tony Hsieh, Zappos CEO[33]: We also fire people, whether we didn't do a good job of screening them during the interview process or if they changed… If we hired someone that was humble [and] for whatever reason three years later they're no longer humble then we will fire them… Usually this type of thing we find out in the first 90 days. And so our turnover is pretty low once people make it past their first 90 days. But we do fire people if they're not living the core values.
Bob: It takes 91 days to really know the employee (formula: days to become a permanent employee + one). We never know about bad hires until it is too late.

[33]Personal interview, August 7, 2008.

Privilege

Part of my job is to keep challenging colleagues, asking questions, sharing ideas. If an idea has merit, maybe it'll stick with them and it'll grow. I very rarely give a directive, I seek consensus. But in rare cases when people don't find any consensus solution to a major problem, I give a directive saying: "Thank you for input! But now, I am invoking 'Executive Privilege.' If things go wrong, it is now on me. If it goes right it is on you." Then, I need to spend the time with them to give them all the information I can so that they can say, "We don't agree with him but he's fair." Because once I get fairness, I can get respect. If I make the decision without telling them why, I risk losing their respect because I didn't establish fairness (see Love vs. Respect).

When at Sea Smoke we were heading toward troubles in our marketing, image issues, or anything that could change the perception of value, I would sit down with Victor and say: "Victor, very rarely you would see me give an executive order. I'm just on the road toward giving an executive order but I don't want to. But what I'd like you to do is to look at this particular issue and find a way out. How would you handle that? If you can't find a way out, my executive order will be to execute plan B." My experience is that colleagues always find a way to solve the issue on their own.

Round-Table

Brian: Part of giving up your ego as a leader is recognizing what you can't see from the top, so to speak. Standing at the summit, you may be able to see across the ridges that separate marketing from sales from engineering. And that's a virtue. But you can't see what's going on down on the valley floor—it's too far, and things get in the way. And that's a failing.

From the top you can facilitate communication across the lines that divide one department from another, and remind everyone what the business's goals and vision are. But if you don't let those on the front line incorporate that insight into what only they know, you're missing out on at least half of the insight and data available.

Product Development Tube

I asked the company to visualize a long tube—a year long. After we all agree on what products will be developed and the order in which they will start, we place those ideas in the tube. Once they are in the tube, they cannot be changed (unless the engineering VP agrees). A seemingly simple change could cause a start-over situation. No changes, commit to your ideas before they are placed in the tube. It takes a year for the ideas to flow through the process and become products.

We had trade shows every September. The sales people always wanted a slew of new items to show, which meant time-consuming mock-ups by the development team. Once, when the salesmen were told they would not get their new pet project by the tradeshow and it would be two months later (due to where it was in the tube), they screamed, "That is two months late!" I quietly explained that their pet was not two months late… it was ten months early (meaning they would have their developed product exactly as it was scheduled, a year later).

You can tell a well-run company by looking at the engineering parking lot. If the cars are gone at 5:05 p.m., you are in trouble. The development team is burdened with all of the logistics and technicalities of getting the product finished (the sales staff usually have the problem of scheduling a golf game with the customers). This bothered me for years as I saw the good engineers leave the company—not at 5:05 p.m. but forever. I thought that the development people deserved a life like other departments. So, I created the tube concept and scheduled it so one new product would go to the production line at the beginning of every month after being in the tube a year. The engineers could now schedule the project (and their home lives). The turnover in engineering was big in Hong Kong, we were losing the good people. After we added discipline (the tube), we started getting the best engineers in Hong Kong coming to us, because they could have a home life as well as being challenged professionally. They saw leadership.

All was not perfect! Sometimes we had to have the development team work long hours to get products for tradeshows. So, every staff meeting we would discuss "Running the horses." This was a conscious decision to schedule longer hours for a limited period of time and all of the managers were in on the discussion so they would be aware of the sacrifice made by the development team (see also Real Life).

Round-Table

Isaac: 9-to-5 behavior is a sign of disengagement, which comes about because the environment doesn't care about employees' fundamental needs. One's personal and social life are parts of these needs. Companies that don't care about these needs—because they care only about their own—don't have engaged, self-motivated people. Hence, they must resort to extrinsic motivation—carrots and sticks. Some people can go for long time and put in long hours in such an environment. But work stress is hard—not to mention stress at home from one's absence. Most employees either disengage and start working 9-to-5 or they leave.

Question, Asking the Right One

Employees' biggest fear is that somebody will take a negative approach to their decision making. Get thicker skin through intellectualizing the problem and removing the person. All I want is to understand the logic of how they got to their decision. I ask a lot of questions just to educate myself. But I'm not to make the decision in their place; I have no ability or skills on their specific problem. A leader, however, has to make the decision when it is his or her "monkey" or when no one else takes the problem. I always try to place the monkey on the correct back. When the problem surfaces, ask: "Whose monkey is it?"

Quitting

In Radica, in China, when a good employee wanted to resign, I'd say: "You play a very important role in our company and I'd hate to see you leave. Why do you want to leave the company?" And he would answer that he is going to a better company. In China, "better company" translated then to 10 cents an hour more.

So I'd say, "Let's have a cup of coffee," so we could go to "neutral turf" away from my desk. We would sit down and chat a little bit: How's this and how's that and how's your family. Then I'd say, "There's no way that I'm going to convince you to stay?" And he'd reply, "No, I'm going." So, I'd say, "Well, here's my card. If after 30 days you find out that it's a better company, then I want you to call me, because I'm coming too." And he would say, "What? You're the owner!" But I'd continue, "No, if it's a better company, I'm coming too. And if it takes you 60 days, then I want you to still call me. But after 60 days, if you find out that it's *not* a better company, I want you to call me because I'm holding your position for 60 days. Okay? I'm going to leave your seat open here for 60 days. So you think about it."

Well, many found out that the 10 cents an hour didn't matter because their life became hell. So they came back where they could have a happy environment. The culture was the basis of the low turnover and my main argument was to make them think about it. The average turnover in our industry in China was 33%. We had 2%.

Quitting, Part II

In China, if you admit failure, you have to commit suicide (not literally). If you quit for 60 days and then come back to the company, that's failure. So you come back, you humiliate yourself. So this is a tough cultural issue to break. I had one person come back, a good one. He came back and he said about the company he had joined, "The guy's a dictator, they fight all day long, it's absolutely horrible. Here you trust everybody, there's no fighting, no yelling."

Once that one person comes back, you break the ice. Now you use that example to show the rest of the team. So, then I had six people come back. I'd say, "Well, you know we've had a Manager of Marketing, we've had a Director of Information Services, we've had a Vice President of Engineering, we've had all these people come back. Why? Because when they went to these places, they had no lives, they had to work till midnight, had to work Saturdays and Sundays and didn't get paid for that. I'm trying to save you from going to a company where they're not going to respect you. Why don't you think about those things and maybe contact one of the people who came back?"

And then you start to get a one or two that would withdraw their resignations right away. Then you start to get to the snowball effect and the turnover rate plummeted.

Reaching the Pinnacle

The worst thing that can happen to a company is that you believe your own bullshit. You really don't want to believe your own bullshit. You want to stay humble and figure out where you are in relation to your competition: "Yes, we're good–but are we the best? Maybe not. So what can we do to get just one percent better?"

In Sea Smoke, at harvest time, we drink wines from Burgundy, the motherland of Pinot Noir. My goal is to get everybody here more experienced about the outside world so that we don't just get focused on just what we do. What we do should be in context with the world so that we have a broader view of where we are in relation to competition. I think we're really good in California but we are not at the pinnacle of the world. So, to humble ourselves, we need to drink really good wines and experience these different styles, to give maybe to somebody a spark or an idea of another way to blend or another way to improve our quality.

Readers of Bullshit

In the wine sector that we are operating in, especially at this price point, clients are not just buying a brand. They are buying a relationship with the brand which at the end of the day is a relationship with the people behind the brand. And if the words and emotions of the people behind the brand ring hollow, clients are very good bullshit readers. Everybody here at the end of the day is a salesperson. Everybody in the company is a brand emissary. The internet can spread negative comments instantly. Be incredibly honest!

Round-Table

Brian and Isaac: As we mentioned above, USAA's Robert McDermott saw his management approach as an extension of the Golden Rule. As he put it to us, "When people serve others, they are living the philosophy of 'love thy neighbor' and that's their psychic income." McDermott also liked to hand out a printed page that had versions of the Golden Rule as it was expressed in all major religions. He wasn't preaching, he told us, but he believed that the benefits of serving and loving others were universal. This was not "mere" altruism, however. USAA's ethos of caring about its employees and asking them to care about their customers led to lower employee turnover, lower customer churn, and job- and customer-satisfaction ratings that were at the top of their industry for decades. Customers, too, know when your employees are just "phoning it in," and it affects the perception of your entire business.
Victor Gallegos,[34] Seasmoke's long-time general manager, put it this way: "The essence of what this vineyard is transcends vintages, transcends producers. You know when you drink something from this vineyard. To reach this irreproducible quality you need everyone in the company to be emotionally involved and share this vision. … Perhaps it can be done with large budgets, but 'money can't buy you love.'"

[34]Personal interview, September 16, 2008.

Jean-François Zobrist[35]: "Everyone has to seek and serve the love of his client." By client I mean an outside one as well as a colleague whom one is supposed to serve. Indeed, the only reason for an employee to be fired in FAVI is the non-respect of this vision and of some unwritten values that define FAVI's culture. Only three have been fired in 30 years including a quality manager who said that he had better things to do than to talk to workers about their problems.

[35]Personal interview, April 8, 2005.

Real Job of the CEO

The CEO's number one job is not protecting the business assets. It's not profitability. It's a human issue, which comes under auspices of morale. It really deals with the culture that allows people to have freedom, work together, and communicate together, which creates an environment where people can enjoy their own success and want to be there. Your priorities as CEO are:

1. Morale
2. Protection of corporate assets
3. Profits

So many CEOs get this wrong by putting *profit* before *morale*. Look at the history of companies like United Airlines and American Airlines, which put profit before Morale.

Round-Table

Robert Townsend[36]: If you're running some part of a company, a few useful questions to ask yourself are these: Are my people excited? Are they energetic? Are they creative? Are they free to make mistakes? And if not, what's chaining them? What's restraining them? What in the organization can I get rid of that will free them to be as creative and energetic and exited as they can be?

To me, the answer has always been the same in all the organizations I've worked in. There is a structure that has just grown up in the organization that is tolerated by everybody. In many cases, this structure is still growing. What it does is impinge on the lives and the energies and the creativity of people… The PR Department, the Human Resources Department … the Management Information System Department if unrestrained, will impinge on the activities of your people, interrupt

[36]*Reinventing Leadership*, *ibid.*, pp. 111–2.

them, force them on committees they don't want to be on, force them to write and respond to memoranda they don't want to deal with, force them to attend meetings they don't want to go to. This kind of activity chains people's spirits and makes it difficult to remain energetic. One of the leader's jobs is to free people from their burdens and get them focused on the vision of the company.

Once they're focused and energetic and excited, the need for control almost disappears. They're doing their thing. They know what's expected of them, they're being rewarded, their progress is being measured, and the feedback to them is up-to-date and frequent. This frees the leader to concentrate on the horizon and the obstacles and opportunities that are looming ahead and to be thinking about the next vision.

Gordon Forward[37]: Nobody asks a CEO to be a saint. And so he may be a good strategic thinker he may be terrible with his people. If he's terrible with his people, the best thing to do is give him a promotion to chairman or something so he can still be part of the strategy.

[37]Personal interview, September 25, 2007.

Real Life

Part of the culture in Sea Smoke is—you have a real life. You're not at work on weekends (see also Saturday Off).

Round-Table

Isaac: Carlos Ghosn, the CEO of Renault and Nissan, once said that the hardest task for him once he became the CEO of Nissan was to make people take one more day of vacation.
Bob[38]: Ronald Reagan used to send his [White House] staff on Christmas home so they can be with their families. He'd say "You don't need to worry about me. You guys need to go home and take care of yourself."

[38]"The Rarest Commodity Is Leadership Without Ego," Bob Davids TEDxESCP talk, February 24, 2012, https://www.youtube.com/watch?v=UQrPVmcgJJk, accessed May 22, 2017.

Reporting, by the CEO

I would write to Robert Townsend—a Radica Games board member and chairman of the compensation committee—three documents every year: my resignation letter, executive compensation plan, and succession plan.

I would give him my resignation letter and add, "All you have to do is take it out of your pocket and tell me you accept it."

The second document was an annual detailed report on my ideology for the compensation within the company. More importantly, I had to discuss with Townsend the executive compensation. He didn't like disparity. He wanted more people to make money. He didn't want a big disparity between high levels. I made less money than the CFO. Why? Because I put it in the business plan. Townsend asked, "Why do you pay yourself less?" I said, "Because I will get my compensation from the equity." I don't want to be perceived as the one taking. I want to be perceived as the one giving. Now, I pay the CFO this compensation because that's the market. But because he doesn't have major equity in the company, it doesn't make sense for me to take more money than him. I will get my money in the equity.

The last document Townsend demanded every year from me was a written succession plan. When I asked why, he said, "If you fall out of the sky and the airplane hits the ground, I want to know what you—not anybody else—thinks the company should do. Tell me what should happen to the company if you crash in an airplane, what to do, who should do what." He added, "You know more than anybody about this company. Don't make the board guess what we should do. You prepare it in advance, in writing, one page. If you can't put it in one page, you don't understand the problem" (see Trick Question). I told him that if the problems were many, I would add a second page. He said, "Put the important stuff on page one—I will not read page two."

Responsibility, with Authority

The number one thing in my companies is that nobody ever got in trouble for making a mistake. You only get in trouble for not making a decision. Decisions and mistakes are the opportunity for growth. The problem I had was getting people to willingly take the monkeys, to make the decisions.

People would say, "Oh, I can't." And I would reply, "But this is the opportunity to grow. My job is to give you the opportunity to make decisions, because those decisions are your growth path. It's when I take those decisions away from you that I steal your growth opportunity. So you should be willing to. Authority comes to those who steal it. You run out and take as much as you can, and you go out and do your best, and if you succeed inside the company, you're the one who gets promoted." So, it all starts with training them to take responsibility.

My job is to prepare them for internal growth (see Growing, from Within). And the way you do it is giving them decisions. For them to make the decision, you have to match responsibility with authority. Any leader who doesn't consciously perfectly match authority and responsibility is a non-leader. If you give them the responsibility to get something done, you better match that with the perfect authority. If you give them the authority to do it, you better match it with responsibility. They must be perfectly matched at every single step and it is the leader's job to do that.

The Right Quality

Visibility is key. You can't fly blind. That's why we have financial models. But when we do business plans, we never say, "How are we growing profits or growing revenues next year?" It's: "How are we improving quality next year?" And we are making adjustments on the run based on doing the right things for the quality and the brand. Profit seems to follow quality (see Hands, Ripping It from Yours). Get the product quality right!

Risk

Most people are afraid to be on the cutting edge. In engineering, we say there's the leading edge and then there's the bleeding edge (where you can get cut). The bleeding edge is when you are out there taking big risks. Most situations a true leader encounters are the ones with high risk.

I went to China. I had no experience with different cultures; I had never been in those situations before. So, in every situation that came up, the only tool that I could use was common sense. Common sense is for doing something that nobody has ever seen or done before. And to be out there, exposed, in front of all those people and all those issues, you had to have confidence, but more importantly, you had to have lightning-fast common sense. Common sense has a forward-looking component to it. You expect where each step will lead you; look as many steps ahead as possible, like stacking up the dominoes to watch them tumble down. People only look at the first domino; they do not peek around to see how many or how fast the dominoes will fall when they tip the first one. Evaluate all of the dominoes behind that you can before tipping the first. So you would see the situation and you'd say: "That step means this and the next step means that and now we're going to do X." Staff would say, "Well, we've never seen that before." And I'd reply, "Neither have I. But it makes sense, let's do it. It's common sense. Let's just do it."

One of the first traits I see when I meet someone is their common-sense level; I am very sorry to say that I do not see many people with forward looking common sense. When I see people who do have this level of common sense, it really takes me aback, because I don't need to waste time, they get everything quickly. We usually bond on this ability to deal with new, unusual situations and to use common sense to get a great solution. We could describe this forward-looking skill as *anticipation*, a necessary natural skill for a leader.

Running to Your Enemies—CU Stick

The CU stick (pronounced "koo-stick") is an American Indian stick that symbolizes you and your family. It may have feathers and maybe a bone from something you caught. The CU stick is the symbol of who you are. And the bravest thing an Indian can do is to take the CU stick and walk up to his biggest enemy and lightly touch them. When you take the CU stick and you lightly touch your enemy, you take their power away.

So, in a conflict resolution, I do the same thing: I run to my enemies. But you just walk up slowly and you talk to them. And you may say something like, "We're having problems aren't we? Why do you think that is?" So I try to disarm them. Main thing is: attack the problem quickly. Go to your biggest problem right away. Go to it fast. And just touch it with your mental CU stick. Because once you're standing there and are able to ask them a question—just by the act of asking them a question—you take the power back.

Saturday Off

Read Dr. Freudenberger's *Burnout*,[39] a must read if you can still find it. I will give the "take-away" from the book.

Hard work and long hours never hurt anyone, but monotony will kill you. When I arrived in Hong Kong, there was a British tradition hanging on that everyone should work 5.5 day/week (half day on Saturday). Because of the book *Burnout*, I wanted to change it. I saw monotony setting in (look at a Hong Kong shop-keeper who is at his counter at 9:00 a.m. and still at 11:00 p.m., dazed look on their face from monotony). I explained the request and took a vote of the 18 managers. One manager voted "no," so no change. I asked, "Why?" She said, I was stealing something from them. I asked what and she had no answer. This went on for 6 months. She was the accounting director so I asked her to find how much I was "taking"; she could not find anything. After I started to figure out the local culture (money is *everything*), I asked her in front of the meeting how she got to work on Saturdays: "Car, taxi, bus, train?" She said, "Train, but taxi when it was raining." I asked her how much she spent coming to work on Saturdays and to multiply that by 50. She instantly voted "yes."

One employee told me that they could cheat me by getting Saturdays off. I asked, how can they cheat me? He said that he would go to the beach and play sports and get tired by Monday when he returned to work. I said, "Perfect! I want your body tired and your mind fresh!" I'm not sure he ever understood.

---

[39] H. J. Freudenberger and G. Richelson, *Burnout: The High Cost of High Achievement*, Garden City, New York: Doubleday and Company, 1980.

The Secret of Becoming a CEO

People don't learn from doing things right. They learn from doing things wrong. So the more things you do wrong, the faster you learn. The trick in life is not to make the same mistake twice.

I had one session with one of the Chinese managers, whom I wanted to take charge of the China factory—he wouldn't. I said, "Do you ever want to be a CEO?" And he says, "Yeah." I said, "Let me give you the secret." And he takes out his pen. I said, "Make more mistakes than anybody else." "In China, you can't make mistakes right?" I said. "No, if you want to be CEO, make more mistakes than anybody else—but don't make the same mistake twice. Then you'll be a CEO. If you don't make mistakes, you can't learn. I get to be CEO because I made more mistakes than you. Don't be afraid to make mistakes." The man took the factory general manager job.

The Senses, Influencing Them

Design in the greater sense is creating "the Perception of Value." The perception of value is the final step a person takes just before a purchase—taking money out of their wallet for a product or service. Design appeals to the five human senses and can influence senses to assist a person in thinking there is value, leading them to complete a purchase. Designers can influence the effect of light, shape, sound, feel, taste, fashion, trend, and other stimuli. Design's function is to convey quality equal to what a person wants to spend.

At Radica, we had 18 designers in our relatively small company. Our two big competitors had two designers. We would lead in innovation (see Listening and Ideation and Shotgun Innovation) which I consider the most important ingredient to be a market leader. Design is too complicated to cover in a book like this; it is a subject for another time.

Sharing Gains

In private companies, giving up 1–2% of equity to the employees never converts to cash. When the Camelot period is over (see Utopia Doesn't Last), that 1% somehow gets wrangled around and employees end up with nothing. They spend 15 years and end up getting nothing. So I'm cutting through all that to the chase. I'm giving them bonus money every year and tell them: "You're probably a better investor than I am. So here is the money and invest it the way you like. Don't trust me. Trust yourself. Go invest for yourself. And don't think that I'm your savior, because I'm not."

In my younger years, I took equity in many companies I worked for. And out of all those deals that I did with small equity, how much I did receive out of all of those? Zero. (Note: Those 1–2% shareholders can destroy a sale of the company by opening it up to lawsuits from small shareholders.)

Sharing Vision

A leader can never be sure that everyone owns his vision! This comes under the topic of motivation: One human cannot motivate another and all motivation comes from within. So, employees "buy" the vision on their own after their motivational barriers are down by virtue of the culture and leaders' subordination. It may take several communications on the part of a leader before an employee takes the vision. He has to keep trying.

Shoeboxes

Si Redd told me to run the business out of a "shoe-box." We will spend everything in the world on what it takes to make great wine and we will spend nothing to house it. That is just ego money and there is no sense in it because it will never come back to you (see also Winemaking Isn't a Hobby).

Once, Si instructed me to locate a larger building to house a rapidly growing IGT. I found the right-sized building and when I led him to the front door he took three steps and said, "Let's leave." I asked, "What's wrong?" He said the carpet was too nice and our customers would know that we would be overcharging to pay for these luxuries. I convinced him to get the building. He was always focused on what the customer perceived as value and we were the custodians of the money they spent with us. Like a salesman driving up in a Roll Royce. Be careful!

Shotgun Innovation

The innovation that was important to us was products that will sell. Most companies hire out innovation. Hasbro and Mattel come to mind. They have a network of outside "inventors"; they basically use a "shotgun" approach: throwing shit (spaghetti) against the wall to see if any sticks (see also Ingredients and Inventory). I used *ideation* meetings to produce corporate products from inside the corporation in a disciplined manner; we never took an idea from an inventor (see Listening and Ideation). Phil Jackson[40] at Hasbro told me every time I saw him that no other company could do what Radica was doing—he was right. He was shocked when we had the mega-hit with *Draw Poker* and followed it up with *Bass Fishin'* (and later with *20 Questions*, an early artificial intelligence game). Because of being the first company to do back to back hits, Hasbro contracted us to put the Hasbro line-up of intellectual properties (*Yathzee*, *Monopoly*, *Candyland*, etc.) into electronic form.

The ideation meetings were really started to get the team to work together so that everyone knew how and where the products were developed and could "buy in" to them. They also saw (when put under the gun) how tough it was when they were put on the spot to create. In other words, we had team cohesiveness because everyone was involved in the process and gained respect for all those who contributed to create (No vacuum, everyone got to see how we worked).

It is important so that the team can work together and remove internal friction. Innovation has to be transparent and disciplined. It is critical that the culture is maintained and everyone is on the same page.

[40]Head of Marketing and Product Development at Hasbro Games division.

Round-Table

Isaac: Innovation is described in many large corporations as a must-win-battle. Yet, most can't win. They invest huge sums in their R&D, which is plagued by the same bureaucracy as the rest of the corporation. Then, they resort to buying innovations from smaller companies or just acquiring innovative companies outright. They must do all that because their mistrust- and control-based cultures kill innovation. Silicon Valley giants are no exception.

Gordon Forward on his experience in the R&D of a traditional steel corporation[41]: All the steel companies in the U.S. were doing the same thing. They all had this research center [and] good ideas were dying there every day... It was very difficult to get [R&D people] over the wall and into production... [Production people] didn't want you messing around with their process. They just wanted to run the plant as it is, don't change anything, don't screw around... We had a few small successes but it was like pulling teeth....

I like this definition of engineering: Scientists discover the way the world is; engineers create things that have never before existed. It's all about taking this science, knowledge and creating something real that never existed before... I wasn't interested in research for research sake. I left.

[41]Personal interview, September 25, 2007.

Size

I'm not sure growing a company just to grow is good. I think the quality of product and the quality of life are something to go after. Size doesn't always matter (see Success and Fun).

Round-Table

Isaac: John O. Whitney, argues that growth, at least organic growth, must be fed—not forced:

> Growth for growth's sake is the fountainhead of disaster. Even if growth for growth's sake does not inundate the balance sheet with debt, it suborns judgment as the spate of restructurings, divestitures, and downsizing … testifies. [Moreover,] economic growth, while important—crucial in the long term—is only one form of growth. An organization can also grow in terms of its institutional learning. Its members can grow in terms of their skills, knowledge, insight, and judgment. Happily, there are no limits here. These require neither scarce nor finite resources. Moreover, this noneconomic growth is essential to successful economic growth and requires as much attention from its leaders. Nowhere has it been written on tablets of stone and hurled down from the mountain top that a firm must grow in revenues by 15 percent every year and return an annual 20 percent on equity. There is a season for plowing and a season for harvest. But without proper attention to noneconomic growth, the droughts will be frequent and severe.[42]

Mencius, a philosopher of the Confucian School who recorded the thoughts of Men Ke, a famous educator, passed this idiom, well-known in China: "You don't help the [rice] shoots grow by pulling them upward." True and sustained organic growth is fundamentally a consequence of the organizational culture that a leader has built.

---

[42] *The Trust Factor*, *ibid.*, p. 56.

Gordon Forward[43]: One president of a steel company similar to Chaparral said to me, "Gordon, I've always admired what you do but I'd never do it because I'd feel uncomfortable with radical change." But I'm comfortable with change. I love it! How do we build strategic advantage in our business by understanding the changes that are coming, like changes in equipment and in the marketplace? When I was starting Chaparral, I asked questions like, "Who do you think is going to be our best competitor in 25 years? Is it going to be a new material, a different country?" And this president said: "That stuff really baffled the hell out of me—how we roll with the punches. I just want to run the company." But I said, "That would drive me nuts. I don't want to run the company. I want to grow it!"

My major concern as CEO of a smaller company of 2500 people was, how do we grow and not lose it [our culture]? What happens if we grow either through acquisition or through whatever? And you can lose it. And sometimes, the "it" is not good and sometimes it is but for us it was good. It was key to our development as a company [And how did I solve this puzzle?] I left the company and we sold it! (laughing) It just got sold. The little company that we started sold for $4.2 billion.

[43]Personal interview, September 25, 2007.

Size and Fun

The fun of a business tends to be inversely linear to the size of the company. The bigger you get, the less fun you have and more headache, and the culture starts to fall apart. The perfect number may be 200. After 200, it really crosses a threshold. When you get past 200, then you have to have another level of management come in and then you get into the vice-president stuff (see Fun Killers: Vice-Presidents).

Round-Table

Isaac: Bob credits his Caltech class for his first awareness of the issue of company size. Interestingly, somewhat earlier, in the 1960s, Bill Gore who built a freedom and fun culture in W. L. Gore was thinking deeply about it. Below is what he wrote in a memo distributed to company associates[44]:

> Cooperation between two people is relatively excellent … With increase in the number of cooperators, communication becomes more complex, less efficient, and limitations arise in the kinds of possible communications. A precipitous drop in cooperation appears as the group size becomes large enough so that everyone no longer "knows" everyone else. At this point one hears the "we" decided, or did, or believed, etc., become "they" decided, etc. This precipitous drop in cooperation is difficult to forestall in groups larger than about 150 persons. Beyond some such level, it becomes necessary to impose rules, regulations, procedures, and the like that dictate how the cooperation shall be done….
>
> One desirability of the good society is that each human has the opportunity to maximize his accomplishments. Enterprises designed to do this are not likely to involve large groups, and usually will consist of not more than 150 persons. If the norm in our society is the utilization of say 10% of our inherent human capabilities, what would be the result if we were able to restructure to enable this to double to 20%?

[44]Bill Gore's internal memo, "The Lattice Organization—A Philosophy of Enterprise," May 7, 1976, p. 4.

Harry Quadracci[45]: One of my most exciting educational experiences was the management conference I attended in Madrid… with 16 other company presidents from throughout the world… For four days, the 17 of us, led by two professors from the Harvard Business School, met to discuss and examine a number of large Japanese, American, European, and multi-national companies to pinpoint and isolate those common factors which have made some companies more successful than others. The companies we analyzed were all of great size, and yet, some have continued their growth without losing the brilliance, productivity, and other factors of success they had when they were smaller. Other companies as they grew lost their vitality and competitive market position, and now are almost a ghost of their former selves.

One thing we did pinpoint is that the single most common characteristic contributing to the downfall of otherwise financially healthy companies is dehumanization and loss of identity of the individual in the name of "professional management." Organization charts, corporate policies, operating procedures, systems, budgets, committees, the organization, return-on-investment, management by objectives and all those other tools of professional management may lead to short-term results. But what is their value if the application of these tools on a long-term basis results in the dehumanization of the individual, so that employees are deemed to be only "workers" and "labor"—something less than whole people?

On the other hand, there are a number of good companies, many United States businesses included, who have managed to grow and flourish and today are the competitive leaders in their field regardless of size. What is the factor of success they share? A high regard for the individual, and respect for the dignity and the rights of each person in the organization. Or in other words, these companies, like Quad/Graphics, are built around individuals and not upon them.

[45]February 1982 issue of Quad/Views, Quad/Graphics' corporate newsletter.

The Smallest Component

The more power you get, the less you can use because as soon as you use the power incorrectly, you lose it all. The power lies in the organization, not within you.

It's like the wall. There are the bricks and the mortar. And in the mortar, there are gypsum, water, sand, and the smallest component of all: lime. Lime provides the glue. So, I'm in the wall, as the CEO, I'm the smallest component. I'm not a brick, I'm not the mortar, I'm not the water, I'm not the sand. I'm that little trace of adhesive that holds the wall together. So, a CEO needs to understand he is the smallest component. He is not the strength of the wall. The strength of the wall is those people sticking together and the CEO's responsibility is to provide the adhesive so they can stick. But CEO can't do the work.

Round-Table

Lao Tzu[46]:

> Why do the hundred rivers turn and rush toward the sea?
> Because it naturally stays below them
> He who wishes to rule over the people must speak as if below them
> He who wishes to lead the people must walk as if behind them
> So the Sage rules over the people but he does not weigh them down
> He leads the people but he does not block their way
> The Sage stays low so the world never tires of exalting him
> He remains a servant so the world never tires of making him its king.

---

[46] *Tao Te Ching* (The Definitive Edition, trans. J. Star), New York: Tarcher/Putnam, 2001, Verse 66, p. 79.

Bob: These words of Lao Tzu need to be on a plaque for all the leaders who think they need a fancy office, a fancy car, first class seats, etc. When they make themselves different, they eliminate their ability to be a leader. In China, I was told the proverb: "If you want to lead someone get behind them."

Spilt Milk Syndrome, Double Bind

This is a valuable lesson I learned at a young age and I still use it all the time. At 8 years of age on my grandfather's farm, I was given the early morning task of carrying buckets of milk uphill from the barn to the house. My grandfather would continue milking while I carried buckets. He would admonish me to be quicker as he needed the empty buckets to continue; he would yell at me to "run faster!"

While I was making the 200-yard run to the farm house, my grandmother would watch me from the kitchen window. When I arrived and would empty the buckets into the creamer machine, she would tell me to "slow down, you are spilling the milk." So, I had my grandfather complaining to run faster and my grandmother complaining to run slower: a classic double-bind. I was confused, as anyone is in a double-bind. I had to find a way to satisfy both. But how? I had to find a way to stay fast and not spill milk. I focused on looking at the edge of the milk in the bucket as I ran, sort of balancing the bucket. I still spilled some milk, but could justify it to my grandmother. I sort of satisfied both grandparents.

The lesson: As the leader, when you run fast be aware of how much you are spilling and control the loss as best as possible. In my business practice now I evaluate the speed I must go to be competitive and try to minimize the loss. Being aware of the cost of the loss vs. the benefit of the speed is something that can be managed—always be aware of what your speed is costing you. In some cases, it is worth the loss to get to market in time. Just always be aware.

Spread of Information

Information is power, so the more information you bring into yourself and you think you have power, the more you stifle the organization and none of us have power.

I saw this in its harshest form in the Chinese patriarchal culture, where they thought if they kept information they kept power; it took five years to break this in Radica there and get everyone to spread the information to those who needed it. Pushing company information away brings power back; holding information causes miscommunication. Lots of gray hairs from this one!

Starting a Business

At Caltech's Leadership Program, there are three things they teach you about starting a business: Do what you do well; know your market—really, really, really understand the market; only accept winning projects. One of the students asked, "But sir, how do we know if it's a winning project?" And the teacher answered, "That's why you're here for two years." And during those two years, you learn how to model a business.

In 1995, I was in Hong Kong, charged with updating the business model for Radica. At that time, I knew already that cell phones would put hand held games out of business and I said, "We're going to be buggy whips. Nobody is going to need us anymore. We've got maybe a five, six, seven year run."

We were the first ones with the Wii technology but finally we couldn't play against Nintendo and Sony. There's no way a little company in Hong Kong could encroach into the market of Nintendo and PlayStation. You must know your limitations. We couldn't make that transition from a small discrete game into a game system: it's a light-year jump. So, if you play out the handheld game market, you only got so many years—it's not a winning project anymore. Every market has a time. Except wine!

Then I started to think. "Do what you do well"—I'm a pretty good wine collector, I'm a really good judge of wine. "Know your market"—I know that Pinot Noir is going to be the thing because it's the ultimate grape. "Only accept winning projects, business model"—it all depends upon the best site.

Thus, I've got an industry where my entry barrier is a piece of land that can't be replicated anywhere on the planet. You can't replicate *La Tâche* from Burgundy. You can't replicate *Richbourg*.[47] You can't. And what's the longevity of the wine business? It goes back to 2000 years.

[47] *La Tâche* and *Richbourg* are two of the most outstanding Burgundy Pinot Noir domains.

What are the chances in the next 100 years that the wine business will fail? I think humans—especially the French—are going to keep drinking wine. I think actually wine's going to rise with the population. It's not like handheld games which are going to die in five years.

So here I've got a business, that all I've got to do to be super successful is to get the right piece of land. If I get the right piece of land, I'm home free. So I spent years to find and buy Sea Smoke's site, which you can't replicate. I have created an entry barrier. Now, you can go check it out: we're the top of the game.

Stifling GM

I loved GM. My mother loved Buick, we always had a family Buick. I won the 1963 Fisher Body Craftsman Guild first prize of a college scholarship (this is how I got into the Art Center College of Design). At graduation, I received offers from every other car company, but I was fixated on GM. I worked at the GM Technical Center as a designer (called a stylist in the old days). The Tech Center was the Hall of the Gods to me. At first, I loved working there (unfortunately, I had to go home at night to a life in Detroit).

The end for me was the unions. They stifled every little bit of competition. I left after 2 years. Now I credit GM's failure in 2008 to the same stifling I saw in 1968.

Stink

You can't have one bit of bad quality out there because you can't get rid of it. If you get stink on your name you'll never get it off. So don't let stink get on your company name. Don't let it happen. It takes four good products to eliminate the memory of one bad product. Another way to say it: It takes nine good engineers to clean up after one bad one. Don't have the bad one; you are better off with none.

Success and Fun

Fun is a corollary to success. Fun goes up as profits and success go up. Fun is sharing the success. Fun should thus be a planned component to success.

We openly talk about having fun and decisions are made with looking at the fun factor, along with improving quality factor. The way to kill fun is to establish "dual standards." Fun also may be the best part of success. I have two requests to new recruits: (1) Never raise your voice; and (2) Have fun every day!

Round-Table

Isaac & Brian: Bill Gore had a habit of visiting new employees and asking them, "Have you had fun today?" If they hesitated, he'd turn to their leader and say: "If they don't have fun, they won't make money." He placed the responsibility for fun on the leaders' shoulders—not on the employees. His goals for W. L. Gore and Associates, set more than half a century ago: "Make money and have fun."

This is a recurring theme among leaders without ego. Gordon Forward of Chaparral Steel tells this story[48]: "When we expanded the plant about four times and the market went down, I called a meeting with my thirty managers and I said: 'Remember our first mission? We're in business for fun and profit. I think we are all getting tired of all this fun because the profit has got to be there. We got to start doing something about this profit before we start having the kind of fun we know we can have.'"

Michel Munzenhuter, CEO of SEW USOCOME, puts it even more simply: "There is no success without employee happiness."[49] While Munzenhuter argues that business success is a consequence of the work

[48]Personal interview, September 25, 2007.

[49]Michel Munzenhuter and Eric Lemaire, *L'entreprise qui libère les énergies : Le management de Perfambiance*, Editions de Signe, 2016.

environment in which employees are happy, John O. Whitney point to the role of the leader in creating this environment: "The job of the leader is to enhance the opportunity for joy." And there are good reasons for this as well as good business reasons for it: "True joy," Whitney writes, "comes from creating something of value." He adds: "People who enjoy what they're doing are more productive."[50]

Bob: Robert Townsend once told another Radica Board member: "This company has more fun than any other company I have been associated with."

[50] *The Trust Factor*, *ibid.*, p. 59.

Suits

A lot of times, when a company is struggling, having a challenge, and the weak CEO thinks that the people he is leading can't come up with their own solution, they hire an outside consultant. Those outside consultants charge a lot of money, so they have to have all the facade of creating value. They bring in all their papers, all of their machines … and suits.

When I was a young designer, I was called into a company to analyze some vacuum-forming production problems. I was consulting for the company on getting the shape of their product right as an industrial designer, not there to solve their production problems. They had spent $50,000 trying to solve this production problem and it hadn't been solved. So they asked me. Fortunately, I had a past stint of about two weeks working for a man on solving some of these problems. I was lucky to have some experience. I looked into it and said, "Oh, you've got the heat on the wrong side." Then, I went back to my office.

At that time, I was charging $100 an hour with a one hour minimum charge. Because I blurted out the answer in three seconds, the most I could charge them was my minimum $100. But they had already spent $50,000 and I gave them the answer in three seconds for $100. I kicked myself saying, "I can't believe I'm that stupid." What I should have done was sit down, analyze the problem, make up a big presentation, take back the presentation, show the answer and charge $1000, and they still would be very happy. But I didn't. I should have learned from the "suits."

They come in and build up a portfolio of all these things they're going to do. Meantime, the people inside the organization have all of these consultants running around, asking questions about what's wrong with the company, all things that are the symptoms of a leader who can't communicate with his own staff. That's why he has to bring consultants in and they have to flower it all up. But basically, all they're doing is asking you the questions that the leader should be asking.

What the consultants find out is that nobody respects the leader. But they will not go back and tell the leader he's no good because then they won't get paid. So when I was at IGT, we started to dislike suits. And we liked our leader even less.

When you bring the consultants in, the people realize that they're not trusted by the leader, and then they start to subvert the leader. So the suits will cause the company to start failing.

Supplier—A Better Dog

I havc a project in Bali and I have a very emotional man who's in charge. He is an artistic, creative designer of world renown. He is fantastic. But unfortunately, as gifted as he is in design, he is equally weak in business. He ran 100% over the budget in two years. So I had to stop the project. He keeps bugging me to restart the project. But I still see that he is really a bad businessman and he's trying to "one-step" me—make me agree on the next small step, and then the next small step, drag you in slowly, get you hooked. A tactic perceived is not a tactic. So, I shut everything down and pulled all the money out. I stopped for two years, with him begging me to start up again. He actually got angry, and the more angry he would get, the more comical I would get. I would laugh about it, joke about the time and the money.

Then, my manager came to me and asked, "Why are you doing that to this designer?" I said, "Well, I had a teacher, one time, old wise guy saying, 'Sometimes you have to make people a better dog.' And what does that mean? I don't like any cruelty to animals, but sometimes you have to punish the animal to get their attention, to train them not to do that thing again. So, I'm punishing the designer financially for doing to me what he's done to me over two years, because I'm trying to make him a better dog."

In this situation, I had a contract with a businessman who was a designer but not a businessman. So I had to drag him, kicking and screaming, into the business world. The only way I knew how to do that was by getting his attention. And the best way to get attention of a businessman is with money—or the absence thereof.

It applies to suppliers, to any businessmen you work with. I try not to do it to subordinates because as a leader, your job is to give all of their power back and support them. Hopefully as a leader you never get to the situation where you have to make someone who reports to you "a better dog." That would imply to me that you're a bad leader because you should have never gotten to that situation if you were a good leader.

Sustaining Growth

Companies can only grow so big as a dictatorship. I call them flashing lights: they're good for a while. Dictatorships can't sustain long-term growth. It's like the lame dog untreated. It dies. You need really good communication in a company to grow big. The CEO's job is to use his power in a benevolent manner to build the culture, communication and the foundation, all coming under the auspices of morale. Communication is a morale issue (see Top Guy).

Round-Table

Brian: John Wooden quotes Abraham Lincoln as saying, "Most anyone can stand adversity, but to test a person's character give him power." And Wooden was aware that a dictatorial style was not unknown among his peers: "There are coaches out there who have won championships with a dictator approach, among them Vince Lombardi and Bobby Knight." But, he had a different approach: "I didn't want to be a dictator to my players or assistant coaches or managers. For me, concern, compassion, and consideration were always priorities of the highest order."[51]

Dictatorships, whether in politics, business or sports, are brittle. Like the tree that won't bend so it has to snap, they always look strong right up until the moment they crumble. And when they do, everyone rushes into point out how obvious the weaknesses were, or should have been. But dictatorships, by their nature, hide and conceal those weak points. That may make a leader feel good in the short term, but in the long term, it makes failure inevitable (see Tired Giants).

[51] John Wooden and Steve Jamison, *Wooden: A Lifetime of Observations and Reflections On and Off the Court*, New York: McGraw-Hill, 1997, p. 117.

The S-Word

Bob Townsend said in his book: "If your product's right, your business would take care of itself. Don't worry about selling your shares." That focus on good product is what we did in Radica.

Every time we would go into a board of directors meeting, Townsend would say: "OK, gentlemen, before we get started on today's meeting, I just want to make sure that nobody talks about the S-word today." And everybody knew that meant "share price." Bob Townsend would never allow us to discuss price of the shares or the volumes, or anything to do with the value of the company. So, every board meeting had to be 100% on how do we build the company, increase the product level, increase the sales, the quantity, the quality, and to build the environment of the company. And if anybody started to talk about share price or the value of the company, Townsend would interrupt and say: "This isn't going to be a discussion or question about the S-word, is it?"

The Tank Factor

The more serious a negotiation gets, the higher the dollar value, the more you need to be aware of the tank factor. When you cancel something and throw it away, you throw it "in the tank." For a really, really, really big contract, no contract is great until it's been tanked (canceled) twice, minimum. Sometimes you walk away from a deal and come back later. For really big deals, you may have to do it multiple times.

I may come back with competition (see Negotiation, Two Tools Of). But it depends, because sometimes you need to make them a better dog and you may let it sit for two years (see Supplier—A Better Dog).

Tap-Dancing Whores

When I was the designer at GM's secret advanced design STUDIO X, I was asked by the Industrial Design Society of America to give the keynote speech at their annual conference in Los Angeles. I decided to talk about creativity. I needed a speech title to catch everyone's attention so I called the designers "Tap-Dancing Whores." I explained that we are "hired guns" who are expected to *create* on demand, just like a dancer who has to get up and dance when the money hits the table. As hired guns, we solve creativity problems when the solutions are needed, not when we feel creative—that's never an excuse.

I broke creativity into two categories—inspiration and perspiration (see Inspiration vs. Perspiration).

It is always nice when we get a "flash" idea and the problem is solved—this is inspiration. We were inspired by a solution. But most of the time this doesn't happen. We then grind out the solution—this is the perspiration.

When inspiration doesn't strike, it takes great discipline to work through the problem as well as the confidence (belief in our education and abilities) to go step by step to find a solution for our clients. I focused on getting one's "mind-set" into being a tap-dancing whore, not a prima donna.

Theory X

If employees are primarily after material needs, it means that they are in bad cultures, bad environments, with bad leaders who cater to these material needs, hoping to motivate people. If people are put into the right environments, they can motivate themselves. I don't think they are a lost cause. I don't think people want to go to "Theory X."[52] I think it is anti-human. The only reason they do is that they have no choice or they don't believe that the alternative is possible.

Round-Table

Isaac: I often get the remark from my executive seminars that people love perks. Of course, they do if the CEO loves them.
Bob: If a person makes this remark, you are not speaking with a leader.

[52]In his book *The Human Side of Entreprise* (New York: McGraw-Hill, 1960/2006) Douglas McGregor coined the term "Theory X" to denote the organizational environment in which people are viewed as inherently disliking work; requiring coercion, control, and direction to put forth adequate effort; willing to avoid responsibility and seeking security above all effort.

Things We Cannot Do

I traveled from Asia to the USA and Europe almost every month; I saw big culture differences. Example: In Asia, I would ask for 100 widgets and then be told that they could provide 82 Widgets. In Western culture (USA and Europe), I would ask for 100 Widgets and be told, "I cannot get you 100 Widgets." There was the underlying difference in cultures. The Asian culture said "what they *can* do," while the Western culture said "what they *can't* do." I decided to "cross" the cultures. When I heard what could not be done, I would divert the conversation to examples: I would say that I could not drink the Atlantic Ocean, I could not throw a train 100 feet, I could not balance my car on my nose, and that I had at least one million more examples of what I could not do... The list would be infinite. But—if I wrote just the things that I could do, the list would be very short and they would not have to listen to my stories. The meeting would then focus on what we could do. When they again digressed and started mentioning what they could not do, I would interject: "Is this going to be one of those long lists of things we cannot do?" They would quickly say, "No, no, we *can* do..."!

Time Horizon

A leader needs to be looking at month to year and beyond. All minute to minute, hour to hour, day to day, week to week, month to month stuff—you shouldn't be dealing with those. The people you hired are supposed to be able to deal with it. If you're doing one single thing of them you are mismanaging your business.

Time to Get Away

I learned from Townsend that when the rough times hit, that is a great time to get away for a while (but be reachable), because it's your team that gets put in your seat when you're gone. The measure of good leadership is the company running better when the leader is away.

Tired Giants

Some command-and-control companies are making big profits. But money is not the only criteria for success: Their employees are usually miserable, just existing without energy. These companies are institutionalized. The "personality" gives way to "boxes." When a company gets fully mature, institutionalized, it has lost the effect of personality. Example: give me a name associated with these companies. IBM? Difficult! People work in "boxes." These companies replace "boxes," not personalities. People with business acumen and personality run from these companies, which become monolithic giants without a personality.

Round-Table

Isaac & Brian: Gordon Forward once said, "We can't treat our business as if it were a large, mature operation that needs to be propped up or pampered. We can't relax and build monuments to ourselves," by which he meant bureaucracy itself.[53] John O. Whitney put it more starkly. He had looked at "hundreds of businesses, large and small, troubled and presently untroubled," and concluded that "about half of [corporate] activities are unnecessary. Put another way: Costs are about double the optimum."[54] Research supports Whitney's conclusion. According to Stubbart and Knight,[55] 99% of large companies don't survive 40 years—they end up bankrupt or acquired before then—and this, despite the myriad turnaround efforts many of them undergo before the end comes.

---

[53]Gordon E. Forward, interviewed by A. M. Kantrow, "Wide-Open Management at Chaparral Steel," *Harvard Business Review*, May–June 1986, p. 97.

[54]The Trust Factor, ibid., p. x.

[55]C. I. Stubbart and M. B. Knight, "The Case of the Disappearing Firms: Empirical Evidence and Implications", *Journal of Organizational Behavior* 27 (2006): 79–100.

As Whitney puts it: "The company cannot afford mistrust. It cannot afford to sap people's energies by requiring them to constantly outwit tar pit bureaucracy. It cannot afford a towering organization structure and stove-pipe functions with the attendant excesses of inspection, supervision, checks, balances, reports, and controls. If it does not unburden itself of this baggage, it will provide full employment for the next decade's crop of turnaround specialists."[56]

[56] *The Trust Factor*, *ibid.*, p. x.

Together, in the Garden

Casey is a gardener in my Bahamas house. He's honest, hardworking, and punctual. He tells me the truth all the time, shows up every day, is never late, and never misses. So I see Casey as a warm, honest, trustworthy, good human being.

One day he asks me, "Can I borrow a hundred dollars?" I gave him a 100 dollars. He comes back two weeks later and says, "Here's your hundred dollars back," and he tries to give me interest. I don't accept either the 100 or the interest, because he has a tough life. When I'm working with him in the garden, we are exactly the same. He's unfortunate in that he can't read, he can't write, he can't count. It doesn't matter that I spent fifteen years in college and he never spent fifteen seconds in school. When we're working together in that garden, we're equal. It doesn't matter his color, it doesn't matter his education. As a leader, I believe that no person is better than any other person. At that time, we are simply two people working in the garden. It's just a respect for humanity and I'm honest about it.

I honestly believe that we are 100% equal. Can I be a CEO on Wall Street? Yes. Can Casey? No. But that's just a different skill set. With regard to what makes us a human being, the essence of us, we're equal. He just had a tougher life, learned a different skill set. But he's no less, no more than me. If a leader of a country or a company can just understand that he's no better and no worse than the people he leads, that he just has a separate skill set, then he can be a real leader. But so many people, they just can't get the fact that having a different skill set, doesn't make them special (ego again). It gives you more responsibility to use the skill set to help the rest, that's all.

I'm not a communist, I'm a capitalist. I just believe that we're all equal and if at the end of the day, my skill set allows me to make a little more money than them, I will make it. But then I have a responsibility, like with Casey. I don't give him a whole lot of money. I give him the market price, plus some. But whenever he has any trouble, I take care of all of his medical expenses, his wife's medical expenses. I do all of that for him, because I was blessed and given a gift.

I'm still a capitalist, but I have enough—now we use the word—compassion that I'm not going to let a man who works with me in the garden, whom I respect, sink. I don't want the government to tell me to take care of him. But I will take care of him and his family and everyone else that's close to me. I will not do it because the government pushes me. Now we're back to pushing the chain (see in Forewords: A Chain). I have never met a government that knows how to spend my money better than me. No government in the world can spend my money for a better cause than I can. I can take care of Casey and a lot of other people, much better than any government. And any government that tells me they're that smart is stupid. No government can take care better than a strong capitalist. They cannot. Now, some capitalists are greedy. And some governments are corrupt and ineffective. So, the fact that there are greedy capitalists is not an argument for allowing the government to take our money to do what we should be doing ourselves for the people around us, to help them stand on their own.

Ton of Money

If the environment is right, then we do the product right and we make a ton of money and have a blast. You can't force making money and having a blast. In Sea Smoke's culture, there is zero tension and there is absolute trust. Everybody trusts everybody to make all the right decisions.

Round-Table

John Wooden[57]: Many leaders stand up and sell "profit," or "quota," or "winning." "Profit," "quota," and "winning" are neither a philosophy nor success but rather what *may* be produced as a by-product, after-effect, or consequence. As my leadership matured, I stopped selling "winning"—avoided even saying the word—and begun selling a set of principles and values that are the prerequisites for achieving *success* as I came to define it….

Bob: I think success for a company is measured in the culture, more than personal achievement.

Bob Koski[58] was founder and long-serving CEO of Sun Hydraulics. Koski took Sun Hydraulics public in 1997, but he never stopped running it for people first. In his 2003 Annual Report to Shareholders, he wrote:

> A most useful way for shareholders to evaluate the quality of longer-term investments in companies like Sun Hydraulics is to gather clues about how a company tends to think and behave. Most people start learning about a company through management reports.
>
> Personally, I learn much more about companies when I can freely communicate with a broad spectrum of employees. It's sort of like listening to taxicab drivers when you want to learn about what is really

[57]*The Essential Wooden*, *ibid.*, pp. 30, 33 (the emphasis is by the authors).

[58]Foreword to Sun Hydraulics' Annual Report, 2003. Reprinted with permission.

happening in the local politics of a large city. Somehow, the printed information in most annual reports does not give me much comfort that I really understand a company. I do not believe that the hard "numbers" really explain a company's potential value. Additionally, I often feel that "management remarks" do not reconcile with how companies are likely to think and behave.

Consequently, if you are, or, might wish to be, a serious 'investor' in Sun Hydraulics, come to Sarasota, Florida, Coventry, England, or Erkelenz, Germany and meet your investment: the people who are the heart and soul of our company.

Top Guy

Only the person with the final decision can control morale—the environment where people can motivate themselves. Vice presidents, general managers, and supervisors cannot control the environment and can only assist creating it (culture). It is the CEO or person with the final word that controls—he is responsible for the culture (see also Real Job of the CEO; Number 2).

Trademarks, Not Patents

Bill Lear had 450 patents. While having a beer with him one night, he told me to never file for a patent. I asked, "Why is that?" He replied, "Patents are nothing more than a written invitation to a law suit." He spent the end of his life defending patents—a wasted effort. I listened to Bill Lear when I was CEO at Radica Games. We trademarked products instead because you only had to convince a customs officer that copy of a trademark confuses the market. That officer could halt an import based on Trademarks and Copyrights. If you try to stop a shipment for patent violation you had to put up a very large bond in case you lost the lawsuit.

The real answer is to patent breakthrough ideas (landmark patents like laser beam). For lesser ideas, get in the market, take the cream of that market, and move on… Let the copiers fight over the dregs of a market. Get in, get the sales, and get out (see Cream).

Round-Table

Brian and Isaac: The benefits of patents for innovation is one of the most entrenched and misleading corporate myths. David K. Levine, an economist at Washington University in St. Louis, asks: "Is it a coincidence that the main accomplishment of the patent system is to encourage rent-seeking behavior?" His answer: "Well, consider that originally the only purpose of the patent system was to encourage rent-seeking behavior. There was no fiction that it was a reward for invention: The king simply granted favored rent-seeking courtiers monopolies over the production of salt, the land in Virginia, or whatever the favorite with the largest bribe happened to desire."[59]

---

[59]David K. Levine, Intellectual Property: Silly or Sinister? *Freeman*, January/February 2011, Vol. 61, Issue, http://www.thefreemanonline.org/featured/intellectual-property-silly-or-sinister.

Indeed, as we detailed in our book *Freedom, Inc.*,[60] only 5–10% of patents are relevant to sales and only 1% of them actually contribute to profits. In fact, when it comes to patents, what really matters is the number of patent citations by others. Other research shows that a portfolio of frequently cited patents does correlate with sales of innovative products. Similar logic prevails for patent citations' relevance to profits. In the late 1990s, IBM held the world's largest patent portfolio. But when measured by citations, its position was less impressive: its portfolio's relevance to profits was lower than that of Cisco or even of a much smaller company like Micron Technology.

[60]B. M. Carney and I. Getz, *Freedom, Inc.*, Crown Business, 2009, pp. 34–35 (revised edition, 2016).

Trick Question

Whenever an executive starts to tell you only good things, you know you're in trouble. I have a trick question to stop the chest beating: "What is your biggest problem right now?" Anything above 6 on my scale of 0–10 gets me involved. So, if the biggest problem you tell me is less than a 6, then we go on with the conversation. But if it's above 6, then we stop. You better focus on this problem or we're in trouble.

T.C.

Bob Townsend would only listen to problems, stating, "Good things take care of themselves." I read in a book that as an executive, there are only three things to do with a piece of paper coming across your desk: (1) Sign it; (2) Throw it away; and (3) File it. I added one more: A tray on my desk labeled T.C. This stands for "Time Cure." When I procrastinated, time usually solved the problem.

Trouble Time

Radica had some bad financial times in 1995 and I asked our CFO how much I had to cut overhead expenses. He said, "63%." "Ouch!", I replied. That was like cutting off 2 arms and a leg. The next day, I went to the China factory, where we had about 5000 people. I called a closed-door meeting with the 18 managers. I started writing on a huge white-board the sales declines by country and product, detailed the costs of running the company, etc. After 7 hours, I asked for help with ideas on what to do. The Chinese staff—who rarely offered any vocal advice—went into a circle of rapid chatter and after 15 minutes, they told me I should cut the overhead by 60%. I quickly agreed because I already knew the number was 63% (close enough). I then asked if they could meet the next morning to give me their plan of how to cut 60% of staff and not kill the company. They agreed and we met the next morning to work out a plan. We cut 60%.

In a board meeting shortly thereafter, I was questioned why the CEO was spending so much time at the factory when the company was in such trouble. I told the board that the factory was key to our quality and delivery schedules and the cultural issues were complex. I said that I had the authority to walk into that room and order a 63% cut in staff, but I would have had an insurrection on my hands in that culture (or any culture). I instinctively took the time to share the information to let them see I was fair, which earned me the respect of their allegiance. The board bought my reasoning and we hit the ball out of the park with the new *Bass Fishin'* game that took our stock from $.75/share to $22.10/share in one year. We rebuilt the staff. The importance of *respect*, *fairness*, *time*, and *information* cannot be overstated.

Trouble with the CEO

You're in trouble with the CEO when he thinks that money is more important than people. If the people, environment, culture, and morale are correct, you have the opportunity to make money. If you focus on money, the lack of morale, the lack of culture will bring you down as a leader. The people in the organization will find a way to get you out. They will. So, you never focus on the money. You focus on the people, the culture, and morale. You build that up, and people motivate themselves. When people make a lot of money, then you're successful as a CEO. But if you start with money, you will not end up with money.

Trout

Rainbow trout never live in ugly places. Fishing is a great way to get business ideas.

Trust and Contracts

At my industrial design company, I would require a purchase order to start working on a project. If the project was big or I doubted the integrity of the customer, I would ask for a full contract.

One customer balked and said, "Contract? You don't trust me?" I explained that the contract was to put in writing what our responsibilities were. I told him if I did not trust him, I would not be talking with him. Contracts are to communicate, not to enforce.

Round-Table

Stewart Macaulay, a legal scholar nicknamed "the Lord High Executioner of the Contract is Dead Movement" in his seminal 1963 article[61] quotes a businessman saying: "One doesn't run to lawyers if he wants to stay in business because one must behave decently." He then explains[62]:

> Undoubtedly, it is true that threats and coercion often are the enemy of cooperation and trust. However, there are social rituals that, to some extent, let us have our cake and eat it too… Most business is carried out by corporations, and the people who work for them have different roles and vocabularies. Purchasing agents, sales people, and engineers often treat a written contract with provisions designed to affect litigation as a mere formality or something the lawyers insist on… Formal documents may be signed by those with power to make contracts, but these documents then are filed away out of the view of those who perform the transaction. Often this is reflected in the battle of the forms. You want to use your proposal form with your terms and conditions buried on the back side. I want to use my purchase order with my terms and conditions that are hidden in the same way. Everyone is kept happy if we execute both documents without ever resolving the conflicting provisions. Contract litigation is rare, and few business people have any direct experience with it.

---

[61] "Freedom from Contract: Solutions in Search of a Problem?" *Wisconsin Law Review* (1963): 777–820, 792.

[62] Ibid., pp. 793–4.

Ultimate Power

Dictators think that they have ultimate power. Wrong! Gandhi had it right: the power is with the people being led. The way it works: first, the leader either asks or takes the power the people offer him. I call this the "first wave." When the power is given by the people, they watch to see if the leader accepts the power for himself or for the people. If the leader takes the power for himself (see Cars, *etc.*), people won't give it to him anymore and it is only a matter of time until the leader is ousted. Inversely, if the leader pushes, or gives, the power back to his people, if he uses the power for their perceived benefit—not his own—an amazing thing happens: the people send a second wave of power. I call this second wave "allegiance," which is *real* power, not surface power.

You only need to study Gandhi to see how he ousted the British merely by threatening not to eat. He had real power.

Uncontrollable Directors

For your board of directors, get proven leaders that you cannot control.

Round-Table

Gordon Forward[63]: Boards are a very funny thing: they're very human, and very fickle. If your company is losing money and you, the CEO, go in and you make a nice presentation wearing your best suit and you've got your Power Points just right and it's just bang, bang, bang and you leave the room, the comment will be: "That was too slick, we're losing money right there. I don't know whether we can use slick people like that." Now, if the company is making a lot of money, you could walk there in your jock strap and sneakers, and say: "You know what you guys, I think this meeting is over, and we should all break for a beer." And those guys would sit there and say: "Now that's the character that built this company. We need this kind of character!" So you, as a CEO, are only as good as your bottom line and boards are so predictable as to what they're going to do. The length of the meeting varies inversely as to the quality of your bottom line. They tend to be shorter when things are going good. And that's all fair: the board should be asking tough questions.

[63]Personal interview, September 25, 2007.

Unions

Unions can be an issue. A good culture rejects unions when there is an egalitarian leader or benevolent dictator (see Sustaining Growth). When the leader subordinates him/herself to the real power of those he leads, there is no need for a union (see Ultimate Power).

Universal People

It doesn't matter where people come from, it makes no difference. People are people. And once you get past all the outside superfluous cultural issues, once you get down to the point where you get to respect that human being, it doesn't matter whether you are in China or Mexico or anywhere else. When the true meaning of a life comes out of that person, they're able to express themselves as a team member in an environment, then they contribute. It's not about where you're from (see also Difference).

Round-Table

Isaac & Brian: Edward Deci and Richard Ryan, psychologists and authors of the leading theory of human motivation, have argued persuasively that certain human needs are universal. But not every culture is equally good at meeting those needs[64]:

> Cultures transmit an array of values, some more compatible and some less compatible with basic needs. We maintain that the more a culture, through its typical style of socialization and the contents of the regulations, ... promotes integrated internalizations [by an individual], the more its members will be in harmony and the more stable will be the culture. In contrast, cultures that either use controlling forms of socialization or endorse goals and values that are unintegrateable tend to foster alienation and anomie and, thus, are inherently less stable. In this way, needs constrain the dynamics of cultural evolution....

Although Deci and Ryan are focused on cultures broadly, their point is equally applicable to corporate cultures. The better they satisfy the universal human needs for relatedness, competence and autonomy, the more stable the organization, and the more successful over time.

64"The 'What' and 'Why' of Goal Pursuits: Human Needs and the Self-Determination of Behavior," *Psychological Inquiry* 11, no. 4 (2000): 227–68, 247.

Visionary vs. Accountant CEOs

You can imagine when you're driving a car on the road, and have your hands on the steering wheel, it looks like the car is going straight all by itself, but it's not. Your hand is constantly making very small corrections, to keep that vehicle on the road. Accountants, on the other hand, are mostly looking in the rearview mirror—reflecting upon the numbers that happened in prior years. They occasionally will look forward, but they spend 90% of their time looking in the past. Visionary leaders, meanwhile, are looking far down the road and making the small corrections to stay on the road. And every once in a while, 1 or 2% of the time, they take a quick look in the rearview mirror (look at the numbers history).

So, the difference between an Accountant and a Visionary is the amount of time they spend looking back. A true visionary sees far ahead down the road, but also just a little bit around the corner.

Round-Table

Isaac & Brian: Robert Greenleaf worked for four decades at the American Telephone and Telegraph Company, now better known as AT&T. He left AT&T in 1964 and dedicated the rest of his life to the study and advancement of what he termed "servant leadership." He notes in his book by that name that a leadership failure in the present is often, in reality, a failure to foresee in the past. And that, in turn, "may be viewed as an *ethical* failure, because a serious ethical compromise today (when the usual judgment on ethical inadequacy is made) is sometimes the result of a failure to make the effort at an earlier date to foresee today's events and take the right actions when there was freedom for initiative to act."[65] In other words, by the time we get around to according blame, the real mistakes often lie in the past, when true freedom of action still existed.

[65] *Servant Leadership*, Mahwah, NJ: Paulist Press, 2002, pp. 39–40.

Greenleaf here points to a profound and little studied aspect of decision making: the non-action. Non-action is often preferred because acting requires effort; it may trigger resistance, while "staying the course" is usually easier to "sell." Yet, leaders—if the term applies—who fail to foresee the consequences of non-action are just kicking the can down the road. Think Kodak.

In politics, on the other hand, very often the opposite obtains: The pressure to "do something" in response to current events is immense, even when a policy response may not be necessary, may make things worse, or would not have prevented a particular tragedy or event in any case.

Leaders in business and politics face a constant tug of war between action and inaction. There is no simple formula for navigating these straits, but it helps, as Bob notes in this entry, to keep one's sights trained on the long term and the big picture.

Visionary vs. Entrepreneur

An entrepreneur has the ability to see the future market—like looking a long way down the road (a bit obvious). A *visionary* sees down the road and around the corner (not at all obvious).

Utopia Doesn't Last

Camelot time is when you wake up and the sun is shining and everybody loves each other and there's plenty to eat and there's drink, and you party all day long. That's Camelot; everything is great! Camelot comes in business when the stars align; the product/service you offer has a great market and profits are good. Camelot periods come and they go; your job in life is to go out and find another Camelot and have as many as you can in your lifetime. But the sun rises and sets on all Camelots, so don't think you're going to go into a situation, and that situation will last forever, because it will not, markets change. So enjoy Camelot, have the best time with it, and then find another one.

I was challenged by a former Radica employee who chastised me for leaving the company; he said everything was perfect, but it changed when I retired. I should not have left the company. He said, "You should have trained someone up." I told him that I trained him up, but he did not run with it. I told him that Radica was my fourth Camelot (it was his first). He needed to go find another and not blame me.

We invented *Bass Fishin'*, did it in handheld form with movement-sensing electronic technology, the very first (a forerunner of the tech that would make the Wii a wild success), sold them for $18.88 at Wal-Mart and sold over 15 million pieces around the world the first year without one dollar of advertising: the most remarkable sales and the highest profitability in toy market history. Now it's Sea Smoke that is in the middle of its Camelot period. But Camelot periods in business come and go.

Wit and the Pleasures of Life

Be a student of life, not just of business. After holding a number of jobs in a number of businesses, I'm coming to see my current job as finding out about the pleasures of life. I started to learn about food and art and music—and wine, of course. It wasn't until I was in my fifties that I became really aware of all the great pleasures of life, and why I should pursue them. But I struggled for so many years to be sensitized, and then to be educated, and then to be experienced. And now, at the ripe old age of 75, I have started to understand both the pleasures of life and the pleasure of helping people in the workplace.

Once you start to evolve as a person, and you have the wit, the ability to learn all these different issues, you also understand better the pleasure of knowing the craft of leadership. Your skill as a leader helps your business and its people thrive.

Winemaking Isn't a Hobby

If you have 1% of hobby in your business, it's 100% hobby. You must know if you have a business or a hobby and be relentless on whichever one you decide; you cannot have a mixture of both; it's hobby or business. At Sea Smoke, the winemaker said it would be great helping me live out my hobby. I immediately stopped and explained the 1% rule. She read my passion for quality wine as a hobby; do not confuse passion for hobby. You can make more profit with passion.

Round-Table

Brian and Isaac: In Sea Smoke Cellars, money is spent only to advance the company's business vision of outstanding wine quality. A former Sea Smoke winemaker told us that every vineyard owner promises that, but then he "puts $20,000 more into landscaping and doesn't allow me to buy an extra $200 wine hose that I need." Sea Smoke doesn't have any hobby expenditures—not for landscaping, and even not for the embellishing the cellar.

Winning, What It Means

What does it mean to be winning? To know that the business plan is working and the culture is working and for me to stay out of the way. Basically, just watch all the young people have a lot of fun as they grow the business. You have been successful when you can sit on the sidelines and watch the team win.

Wives and Dual Ladders

In a company, there are two career ladders. In Caltech's leadership program, they called it dual ladders. One is the technical ladder and the other is the people ladder. The Caltech graduates would work up the technical ladder, reach its peak, and then, they could never make the transition to the people ladder (and the pay that comes with being in "management"). Caltech people would say, "Here's our graduate who is the top nuclear physicist in the world, and he's making $100,000. And here is another guy, the manager and he is making $100,000. The top physicist has 40 years of experience and is 60 years old, and the manager got two years and is aged 25. Who should make the most money? The physicist, of course. But is he? No. So the dual ladders aren't fair. Thus, people want to transition to the people ladder because the biggest earning potential is at its top—you could become the CEO. Caltech, being tired of having their graduates become the top of the technical ladder and not the management ladder, designed a course—on leadership—to help their people transition to the upper—people—management ladder.

I had a young man who headed up my Industrial Design Department at Radica Games, a good designer. One day, he came to me and said, "I want to become the manager of the department." I replied, "Oh, let's sit down and talk: Why do you want to be the manager?" And he replied, "Because I want to promote myself, to grow, to get higher on the ladder and make more money."

So, I drew the double ladder (see Fig. 2) and said, "You are already at the top of the technical ladder and you want to make the transition to the people ladder. With all the technical skills you have, are you ready to give up your career, to go onto an area that you've never tried before? It's a whole different skill set. You really want to be a manager?"

He replied, "Yes."

So I said, "What are you doing tomorrow night?"

And he answered, "I don't know."

I continued: "Is your wife busy?" He is surprised. I explained: "I'd like to take you and your wife to dinner because you're getting ready to

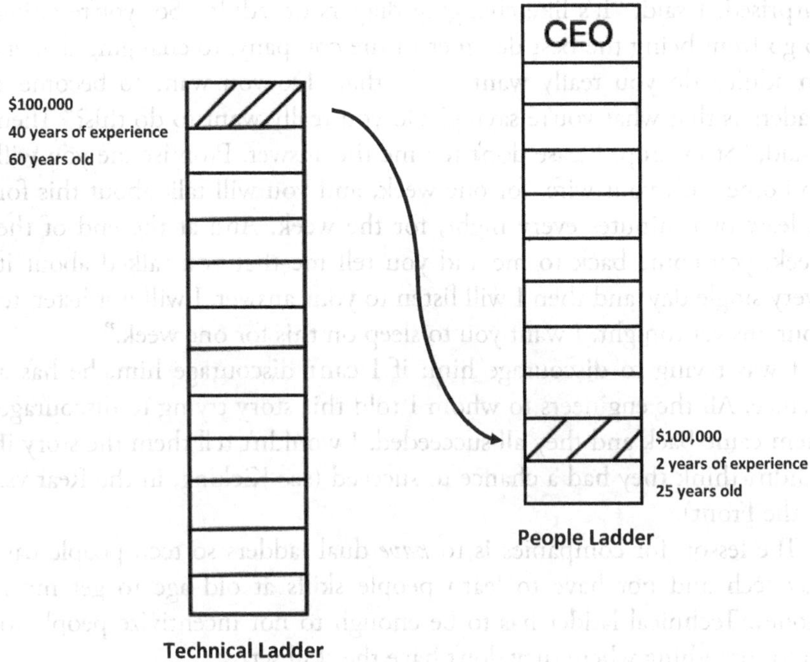

Fig. 2 Dual ladders

make a very big decision. You're at the height of one ladder, and you're getting ready to get off that ladder and go to the bottom of a different ladder. Don't you think you should talk with your wife about a decision of that magnitude? I think you should." He agreed.

Then, we sat down and I pointed to the dual ladders' figure: "You're over here and now you're going into an area, another ladder, where you have shown no skill. You're not showing any aptitude. But you feel like you're compelled to change. I want to encourage that change, but I want you to be fully aware of what you are asking. You're going to go from a position of confidence to a level of uncertainty and you know who's going to have to listen to you every night? Your wife. Why is she here? Because I want her to understand the decision you're about to make."

Then I asked, "Do you know what it's like being a CEO?" He was surprised. I said, "It's like changing diapers on adults. So, you're going to go from being the best designer in the company, to changing diapers on adults: do you really want to do that? Do you want to become a leader? Is that what you're saying? Do you really want to do this?" Then I said, "Stop, stop. Please don't tell me the answer. Promise me you will go home with your wife, for one week, and you will talk about this for at least two minutes every night, for the week. And at the end of the week, you come back to me and you tell me that you talked about it every single day, and then I will listen to your answer. I will not listen to your answer tonight. I want you to sleep on this for one week."

I was trying to discourage him: if I can't discourage him, he has a chance. All the engineers to whom I told this story trying to discourage them came back and they all succeeded. I wouldn't tell them the story if I didn't think they had a chance to succeed (see Kicking, in the Rear vs. in the Front).

The lesson for companies is to *have* dual ladders so tech people can stay tech and not have to learn people skills at old age to get more money. Technical ladder has to be enough to not incentivize people to go to something where they don't have the skill set.

Worries Hang on Your Key Ring

The size of your key ring is the size of your headaches. Si Redd once told me, "Every time you buy something you sell a piece of yourself." Why? Because you have to maintain it, to insure it, to worry about it. So the more you buy, the more you sell a piece of yourself and pretty soon you get so thin you can't do anything. So get rid of all those things and get back to the basics. Everybody has his own basics: it's what he enjoys. Si Redd told me I would "arrive" when I got down to one key. Still working on that!

Wrong Hands

The four critical items people need for success are (in order): (1) luck, (2) talent, (3) brains, and (4) money. Nothing beats *luck*. Use as much as you can find because you cannot create it. I define luck as follows: "When preparation meets opportunity." *Talent* is the next most desired trait for success. Coupled with *discipline* and *risk*, it is an unbeatable combo for success. Next is *brains*. Talent easily beats brains and brains easily beat money. Most people think that *money* leads to success and they are wrong. Money in the wrong hands is a disaster. Hence the old saying: "A fool and his money are soon parted." I see many people with money and they think they have brains. There are way too many of these people and I rarely see them get successful.

Round-Table

Brian: Baseball executive Branch Rickey famously said "Luck is the residue of design," and in a similar vein chess players will sometimes say that great players "make their own luck." In a game, a piece will appear to be in just the right place "by chance," placed there long before its importance could have been calculated. Alternatively, an opponent will blunder in a won position, handing the game back to a top-rated player. But it often takes skill to see the opponents' blunder, and to continue to create difficult problems in a losing position. These are ways of "making your own luck," and in which luck can prove the residue of design. If you place your pieces according to good general principles and the situation that's before you on the board, they're more likely to be in the "right place" when you need them. Preparation meets opportunity, and it can also help create it.

X-it Strategy

If you don't have an exit strategy, your job owns you. At Caltech, they taught us how to build a business model. I added Exit Strategy as the new "first step" in a business model. If you don't know where you are going— you're there.

Sometimes I think it is like the dog that caught the car: What do you do when you get it? In business, what do you do once you are successful? Most people think they are going to lose, but they keep trying. It's human nature. At IGT, I was asked, "When does a $.25 cent slot machine player become a $1.00 player?" This bothered me for a long time. I first figured that when a gambler leaves his home going to Las Vegas he knows he will lose. They say to themselves "I have $500 to lose." How many say, "I am going to go *win* $25,000?" They have a predisposition to lose; they just want a good ride. It is the same when people start a business. They want the ride without having a final goal. Some start businesses just seeing the beginning of the business cycle. Seldom does anyone look at how they will get out of business before they start. I made that mistake a few times. Always look at how you finish one and go on the next.

Radica was advised to go public. This was my exit plan. I could exit by selling my shares slowly as younger people took the leadership role. In 2006, Mattel bought Radica and the exit was complete for many long-term staff. My previous experience of starting and selling companies provided the discipline for me to look at how to get to the next stage of life. Remember, you may only have a chance at 3–4 business cycles: make them count. Interesting that I am now at the 18-year mark with Sea Smoke. Am I at the end of a business cycle?

Epilogue

As the readers have seen from the many references to Robert Townsend in this book, his thinking and example have been very important to Bob Davids. In a way, this book can be read as a tribute to Townsend. It is appropriate then to finish it with a couple of excerpts from his thoughts on the concept of the leader. It comes from an old audiotape that Townsend's widow sent to Bob Davids.[1]

The program's host asks Townsend, "What are some of the character traits of a good leader?" This is how Townsend answers:

> Well, I'll give you a bunch of them. A leader doesn't have to have all of these. And when I get through giving all these characteristics, you'll know more about leadership than you did before, and hopefully you'll be able to identify a leader somewhere in a company and put him in a chief executive position.
>
> He sees mistakes as learning opportunities, not as punishable offences. To him the company is number one. And please, whenever I say "him", you put in "her". I'm not going to say "him and her" all through this thing. Focused to the point of monomania on the company's values and objectives.

[1] *Leadership in Business*, Old Greenwich, CT: Listen and Learn Cassettes USA! Distributed by American Institute of Economics & Technology.

B. Davids et al., *Leadership without Ego*,
https://doi.org/10.1007/978-3-030-00323-4

> He thinks there are at least two other people in the company who would be as good as he is as a chief executive officer. He has very few outside activities, he's got a plain office, he's regarded from below in the company as a winner, he keeps his promises, he promotes from within. The salary gap between him and the next level is narrowing.
>
> He's got small or no public relations activities. He has very little paperwork in planning. He can read people, he can read their eyes: an averted eye tells paragraphs to him. There are few layers of management, there is small staff departments. Openness. He has a performance-based profit sharing, a plan from top to bottom of the company. No policy manuals. No nepotism (except Motorola).

Townsend continues with the list. A good leader, he says, "admits his own mistakes" and "comforts others when they admit them." "He's informal" and "much prefers eyeball to eyeball instead of memos," where today we'd say "email" or even "Slack." The good leader "looks for controls to abolish."

The list goes on: "You enjoy working for him. He's honest under pressure, has character integrity." He has a "proven record of good judgment. Shows guts under pressure. Knows the business and the kind of people who make it tic. People on the shop floor or out in the field respect him. He has respect for all his people. He sees growth as a by-product of the search for excellence, not as an end in itself. He goes where the trouble is to help, instead of calling all the beleaguered people into his office thereby interrupting them."

At this point, the listener might think that she heard more character traits of a good leader than ever. But Townsend is not done. Bob said that he had never been in the presence of an intelligence such as Townsend's. When the reader finishes with the second part of Townsend's answer and takes into account that he provided it off the cuff talking for three minutes, she will see why Bob said it. That is one reason why this book is a tribute to Townsend. "A good leader, Townsend said,

> knows where and how to fire people. He gives honest frequent feedback. He gives credit for good things to others, and says thanks a lot. He has a low expense account and no secrets. He takes the blame often for things that go wrong.

He's usually not a lawyer, a financier, an accountant or an MBA. He doesn't need an employment contract. He's modest. He spends as little time as possible with outside directors and outside activities. He's secure and comfortable under pressure. He delegates all-important jobs and then bites the bullet until they're done. He trusts his people, instead of memos and numbers.

He does dog work when it's necessary. He develops strong convictions. He probably even knows your name! He's visible to the troops. He doesn't need consultants. He's tolerant of open disagreement. He laughs a lot. He simplifies things, makes it look easy instead of complicated.

He is persistent. He is effective. He is tough. He's objective. He's humble, he's decisive. He's fair, humorous, inclusive, available, dissatisfied with his own performance, proud of his people's. He's very simplistic on company values. A good listener. He has a common touch. Probably came from a line background.

He arrives early and stays late. Spends at least 25% and probably 50% of his time outside of his office wandering around. He has no reserved parking place, private washroom or dining room or elevator. He's comfortable with workers and their workplaces. He has no assistants too.

He thinks of ways to make his people more productive, more focused on company goals, and thinks all the time on how to reward them. He's a coach appealing to the best in each, has an open door, he is a problem solver and advice giver. He's hands on, knows how to make people feel important who do dog work. He protects his people from blame and distraction, and carries water for them so they can get their jobs done.

That's it.

That seems like enough.

Index

B. Davids et al., *Leadership without Ego*,
https://doi.org/10.1007/978-3-030-00323-4

9783030003227